7 Baby Steps
to a Ridiculously Reliable
Retirement Income

Peter J. D'Arruda

Investment Advisor and Radio Talk Show Host

Tune in, turn up and drop in as the host of
The Financial Safari, the nation's premier money talk show,
guides Baby Boomers through the retirement obstacle
course, on their way to the finish line, with a goal of
making sure their money lasts as long as they do.

7 Baby Steps to a Ridiculously Reliable Retirement Income

Financial Safari Press
124 Poppleford Place
Cary, NC 27518

Telephone: (919) 657-4201
Website: www.FinancialSafari.com
email: pete@capitalfinancialusa.com

ISBN: 978-0-9859953-0-0

DEDICATION

I would like to dedicate this book to my wife Kimberley, the most loving, supportive, and honest person I have ever known. The beacon by which I sail and the light of my life....
my supercool daughter Carrie who has helped me find good in each day...

...and a good Napa Cab.

ACKNOWLEDGEMENTS

I could not have completed this project without the able help
and constant encouragement of the members of my staff …

CONTENTS

PREFACE

I sometimes don't know if I am a financial planner who does broadcasting, or a broadcaster who does financial planning. I do know this: I *love* my work.

On my first day broadcasting *The Financial Safari* on the radio, my palms were wet and my mouth was dry. I was horrified to think that I could blow it all just by going blank for 15 seconds. I felt as though I was talking to a wall in a very small room. Then a listener called in with a question, and I began to see the audience in my mind. Thousands of them. Behind the wheel on their morning commutes. Jogging with ear buds in. Doing whatever they did that made the gears of their day turn. Instantly, the jitters were gone. The caller had a question about rolling over a 401(k). I knew the answer and was happy to share it. I was no longer thinking about myself. I was back in the saddle, just helping people with their money problems. As Luke Skywalker said in Star Wars after flying his first mission in an X-wing fighter – "It was just like being in Beggars Canyon back home," whatever Beggars Canyon was.

One of the reasons I decided to write this book is because of the thousands of questions that radio listeners have asked over the years that I was either unable to take on the air because of time limitations, or questions that I just could not give enough time to on the radio. After one show, when the topic was one of great interest, the exhausted producer said to me off the air – "So many questions, so little time." He was saying it in jest, but it was true. It is my hope that through the pages of this book, I can give a more thorough response to those questions than the format of a radio talk show can provide.

One thing that hosting a call-in radio show has given me is a feel for the pulse of America when it comes to money. I have a deeper understanding of how people view the accumulation of it, the preservation of it, investing it, and what they want their money to do for them. Immediately after the 2008 market crash, there was a distinct change in that pulse. It was racing out of fear and anger. I could hear the frustration some callers felt at seeing the Wall Street ticker take away nearly half their savings in one fell swoop. The market to which they had pinned their retirement hopes seemed to be suddenly spinning out of control. People wondered aloud why this had happened, who was to blame and whom they could trust. Some of these individuals were approaching retirement and had already established their budgets down to the dollar. Now their ship of dreams had floundered on the rocks and their future was uncertain. It is my hope that the information contained in this book will provide some in-depth direction to those people, and perhaps replace some of that uncertainty with suggestions on how to prevent future disasters and devise a strategy that will provide a reliable income during retirement.

The title, *Seven Baby Steps to a Ridiculously Reliable Retirement Income Plan*, was inspired by two things: (1) The need for seniors to have as steady and reliable an income stream in retirement as they did when they were working, and (2) My little daughter, Caroline, whose transition from expert crawler to shaky toddler was a product of loving direction, the kid's determination, and her willingness to intrepidly take those first few steps into uncharted territory. (My wife, Kimberley, and I have plenty of pictures if you want to see them). Getting to any point in life where we want to be will likely require of us those same character qualities of determination and courage. If we want it, we may have to leave our comfort zone to get it. Just like baby steps, the journey will require acquiring and processing new information along the way. We often need the way shown to us by someone we can trust and someone whom we know has our best interests at heart.

Lately, as I grow older, I have less and less patience for what my high school history teacher used to call, "folks who have their mind made up and don't want to be confused by the facts." But for an honest seeker of truth and knowledge of how to stretch his or her savings to provide a platform for a reliable, dependable, steady paycheck in retirement, I have all the time in the world. I hope that as you read this book, you will do so with an open mind. Expect the unexpected. This is one of those financial books with no other agenda than to pull back the curtain and show you what is there.

Foreword
by Jim Stovall

Financial planning is among the most important work you will ever do as it will affect every other area of your life. I would be the first to admit that money is not as important as your family, friends, faith, or health, but money will affect how you deal with and take care of each of these parts of your life.

I met Coach Pete when he called me to be on his radio show. He heard me speak at a national convention of financial professionals.

As the author of 20 books with several of them having been made into major motion pictures, I am a frequent guest on a lot of radio and TV shows. Of the many hundreds of times I have been interviewed over the years, there are only a handful of interviewers who stand out in my memory. Coach Pete is among those special interviewers I remember fondly. He was polite and professional which you would hope all talk show hosts would be, but, more importantly, he had a real passion and understanding for his topic. Within a few moments of the beginning of the radio show, I knew Coach Pete was passionate about helping his listeners reach their financial goals.

Retirement planning is the most critical element of financial planning as it is the least forgiving area. If someone makes financial mistakes during their college years or when they are a young adult, there is plenty of time to clean up the mess, reverse course, and have a successful financial life.

Too many people today are on a disastrous trajectory with respect to their financial plan, and they have no clue. They will wake up when their retirement financial Titanic hits the iceberg of reality, but by then it will be too little too late. Your retirement planning, along with your estate planning, has got to be done right the first time. You don't get a second chance because if you get to retirement age before you wake up and realize you haven't planned or haven't planned properly, there's nowhere to go. You have written your own financial future in ink with no chance to edit or make corrections.

In these pages, you will find seven simple steps designed to help you reach your financial goals. I emphasize "your" financial goals as the dreams and aspirations you have for your own retirement are the only ones that matter. Retirement is not an age, it's an amount of money. Whether you want to sit on the porch in a rocking chair and enjoy the passing seasons or climb the tallest mountains and hang glide on every continent on earth, it's your choice, and those choices will affect the scope and nature of your retirement financial plan.

Use this book and the wisdom within as your guide to get to your own personal retirement destination.

Jim Stovall
Author, *The Ultimate Gift*

Step One

Take a Good Look Around

CHAPTER ONE

Millions of Baby Boomers Now Coming of Age

"The boomers' biggest impact will be on eliminating the term 'retirement' and inventing a new stage of life... the new career arc."
– Rosabeth Moss Kanter

I remember picking up a copy of *USA Today* a couple of years ago and seeing the headline: "**First of 77 Million Baby Boomers Coming of Age**" and wondering exactly what that meant. Upon reading the article, I was to learn that by "Coming of Age", the writer meant that the generation that was nicknamed "the baby boom generation", because of a spike in the birth rate following World War II, was now – can you believe it? - turning 65. Yep, the generation that invented rock and roll, grew up on black and white television and fought the Vietnam War…the generation that watched Howdy Doody and gave us Woodstock…the generation that put a man on the moon and saw both the beginning and the end of the Cold War… was now ready to retire. And, statistically anyway, they were doing it in the same manner with which they entered the world – with a boom. How would the country adjust to one-fourth of its population stopping work and lining up for Medicare and Social Security?

Officially, to be a baby boomer, you have to have been born between 1944 and 1964. On January 1, 2011, the very first baby boomer turned 65. For the next 20 years, baby boomers would be turning 65 at the rate of 8,000 per day. Let's face it, as this unique bunch gets older, they will likely transform the institutions of aging dramatically, perhaps even redefining what retirement means forever. After all, they have done that to just about every other aspect of American life.

Some who have been looking forward to retirement and now find themselves at its doorstep have that deer in the headlights look, as if to say, "What do I do now?"

Growing up in Laurinburg, North Carolina, I was a Boy Scout. The Boy Scout motto is, "Be Prepared." Some added the words, "and not surprised!" to the motto. That has always stuck with me. As a financial advisor now, it is my job to keep my ear to the ground, as it were, when it comes to matters of financial preparedness. In my work as the host of a nationally syndicated talk show that deals entirely with financial matters, I take questions and have on-the-air conversations with literally thousands of people each year. What I hear sometimes frightens me. Many seniors are in line for a harsh dose of reality, and some are totally unprepared for the shock. Exactly how it will affect the economy is hard to say. Will the country's healthcare and Social Security systems survive the strain? That remains to be seen. One thing is for sure: these boomers, as a societal class, are wealthier and healthier than any generation before and, statistically, as a group, they can look forward to an active old age.

Longevity

Just what is the life expectancy of the baby boomers? Well, life expectancy works in a strange way. Every year you live extends your life expectancy a little further. I suppose the people who analyze this say, "Well, if you've made it this far, you must be made of better stuff than we thought...so we will tack on a few more years." I like the way one octogenarian put it when asked his age: "At the rate I'm going, I'll be 100 before long." The life expectancy of a person who makes it to 65 is 83.6 years. That's an average. It's a bit lower for men and a bit higher for women. Life expectancy gets even better at age 75. If you make it to age 75, then life expectancy becomes 86.5 for men and 87.5 for women.

Health

Baby boomers tend to be more health conscious than previous generations. When an old black and white movie from the 1940's came on the tube recently, however, I found it strange to see how much smoking the characters did. Everyone was lighting up. It was part of the screen play. Not so in twenty-first century movies. Boomers have all but kicked the habit. Smoking is a thing of the past in airplanes, and it's going the way of the wooly mammoth in restaurants. But while that is going on, it appears that not all baby boomers have traded in their burgers and fries for salad and tofu. One poll showed that a higher percentage of boomers are obese than any other group in the country. Boomers came in with a 36% obesity rate, while only 25% were obese in the generations directly above and below them. There is more chronic illness, such as heart disease and hypertension, but those who have it are living longer with it. That may be because of better medicine, at both the diagnostic and the treatment end of things. All things considered, baby boomers can expect to live out the Vulcan greeting made popular by the pointy-eared Mr. Spock of Star Trek fame, "Live long and prosper." At least as far as their health is concerned.

Wealth

For wealth, the outlook is not as good as the health picture. It is true that boomers are wealthier than their parents, but inflation has driven up both prices and wages dramatically on their watch. Real median household income for boomers is 35 to 53% higher (depending on age) than in their parents' generation, and 27% of baby boomers have four or more years of college, making this the most highly educated generation in U.S. history. On the whole, however, baby boomers do not feel that they have saved enough money to cover the costs of retirement for the longevity they hope to enjoy. If retirement starts at age 65, and your nest egg must last another 18.6 years, then as Odyssey said to Houston in the movie Apollo 13, "We have a problem."

What are boomers looking to for support during retirement? Defined benefit pensions have almost become extinct, and 401(k) plans, which could do no wrong in the heady 1990s, went backwards in the 2000s. Home values took a substantial hit when the housing bubble burst. Adding to the uncertainty are higher energy costs, higher health care costs and the effects of the recession that began in 2008 and is still going on at this writing. Baby boomers were raised in affluent times and imbued with high expectations. The first crop of this wave of retirees, however, now faces the ironic prospect of living longer but crimped lives.

Gloom Meets Boom

According to a USA Today/Gallup Poll taken in early 2012, two-thirds of baby boomers say they are less optimistic about retirement than they were 10 years ago. The Insured Retirement Institute recently surveyed a cross-section of individuals from 50 to 66 years of age, and found that only 40% of them were confident of having enough to cover basic expenses in retirement. Sixty percent believed that their retirement security would be worse than that of their parents. Even the pollsters were surprised at how much the pendulum of public opinion within this group had swung toward the negative in just 10 years. One ray of sunshine in the gloom – 74% said that their retirement picture would get no worse, and would probably improve.

When asked from what source their retirement income would come, most of this sampling of boomers, 46%, said 401(k)s, 403(b)s and similar defined contribution plans. Only 37% listed traditional pension programs as their main source of income during retirement. The older the boomers get, the more these programs drop off.

The 2008 market downturn took a toll on wealth; inheritances on average won't be as big and many shop-till-you-drop boomers simply haven't saved enough money to last through their retirement.

Apparently, some of the baby boom generation are the embodiment of the attitude espoused by that dubious spokesman of their youth, Alfred E. Newman of *Mad Magazine* – "What, me worry?" According to Annamaria Lusardi, economics professor at the George Washington University School of Business, there exists a general lack of financial literacy and planning among "a sizable group of the population that has not even thought about retirement." She points out that many people see retirement as a distant stage, even if it's only five years away.

With all that in the wind, it's not surprising that a significant number of those polled said that they expect to postpone retirement past age 65. Does that mean that the old 30-something gang will still be showing up for work at 70-something? So it appears, if they hope to enjoy a retirement that enables them to continue the lifestyle to which many of them have become accustomed. It is a fact that more and more boomers are either working or beginning a second career after "retirement age."

One thing is sure – seniors in the music industry aren't retiring. The Rolling Stones are still together at an average age of 65. Check out this list of "mature" citizens from the top ten grossing music concert tours for 2010:

- Bon Jovi (age 48), #1 music tour with $201 million worldwide
- AC/DC (lead singer Brian Johnson, age 63), #2 (tied) music tour with $177 million worldwide
- Roger Waters (age 67), #2 (tied) music tour with $90 million worldwide from a mid-year start
- Dave Matthews Band (Dave Matthews, age 43), #4 music tour with $72.9 million
- The Eagles (singer Glenn Frey, age 62), #6 with tour with $64.5 million
- Paul McCartney (age 68), #7 music tour with $61.8 million
- James Taylor (age 62), #8 music tour with $50.7 million

Hey, it looks like old age is cool…and profitable!

What's in Store

This flood of seniors and their changing economic status from workers to retired, semi-retired or soon-to-be retired, will change a lot about our culture. Many think taxes will increase. In addition, someone has to pay for the heavier medical care burden. However, there are many possible benefits to having (proportionally) more seniors around. They have one commodity that cannot be overlooked and one that I hear ranks pretty high on the qualifications list of contributing members of society – experience. Boomers have already introduced the concept of volunteering to our culture. Seniors have a great deal of knowledge and experience to share with younger people. Retired boomers will have even more time to become engaged in this way.

The 2011 Social Security Trustees Report has the system running out of money by 2038 unless reforms are made. Proposed reforms include: raising the retirement age, raising payroll taxes and perhaps even revising the benefit formula in a number of different ways. But not to worry, boomers. Most of you are "grandfathered" in (pardon the pun), and the reforms will probably be phased in over several years, so most of you will probably not feel a thing. As to whether Social Security will be here in its present form for your children, however, that is another story.

"A ruthless job market, a suffocating household debt and a shocking decline in the stock market have left millions of Americans feeling fragile and with little confidence they will ever have the money to retire." - *After Fifty Living*

CHAPTER TWO

This Ain't Your Father's Retirement

"Earth provides enough to satisfy every man's need,
but not every man's greed." – Mahatma Gandhi

I was a "honeymoon baby." That is, I was a souvenir of my parent's honeymoon. I was born exactly nine months to the day from when it started. My arrival was a mixed blessing at best. My father, a full time student working on his Masters degree and a PhD in Physics, and my mother, also a college student, needed an addition to the family like they needed a hole in the head.

To say that I grew up in a family of modest means is an understatement. But we never went hungry. One of my earliest memories is that of a large metal can on the kitchen counter stenciled with the words, "peanut butter," in bold government-style letters. Sitting next to it was a plain box marked "cheese" in the same stark lettering. I would learn later that it was something called "government surplus," a precursor to food stamps. It was free, but you had to be poor to qualify for it.

Wants versus Needs

Things got a little better as I grew older, but not much. There was little money in the house. What there was went to pay for necessities like nourishment and shelter. Those were needs. As I remember it, there was never a problem in our home making a distinction between **needs** and **wants**. Needs, I came to conclude, are absolute and gnawingly apparent. Wants are arbitrary and usually frivolous.

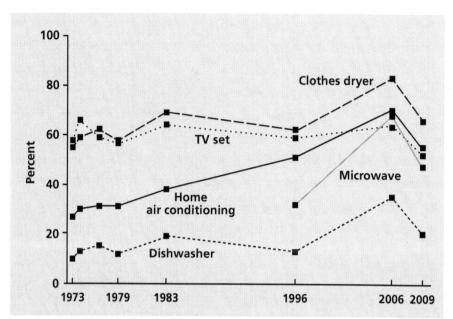

From Luxury to Necessity—and Back Again. Question wording: Do you pretty much think of this as a necessity or pretty much think of this as a luxury you could do without? Source: 1973 to 1983 surveys by Roper; 1996 survey by Washington Post/Kaiser/Harvard; 2006 and 2009 surveys by Pew Research Center.

It troubles me that today's society, especially in wealthy countries like the United States, is defined by its craving for instancy. Baby boomers started the push button era sometime in the 1950s and soon consumers were hooked on instant coffee, instant tea, frozen TV dinners and so many labor saving devices that kitchens couldn't contain them all. Now we are addicts, and we have passed the habit on to our kids. The line of distinction between wants and needs always seems to blur when there is plenty, but usually comes back into sharp focus during hard times.

According to a survey conducted by the Pew Research Center's Social and Demographic Trends project, Americans are rethinking what they can and cannot live without. It used to be that most folks saw such things as microwave ovens, home air conditioning and TVs as luxuries, and now more people see them as necessities. Do you have a cell phone? Could you part with it? Half of those polled said they viewed cell phones and personal computers as necessities. Food is a necessity. You can't eat a computer. Would you go hungry to keep your cell phone? That is the true test, I suppose.

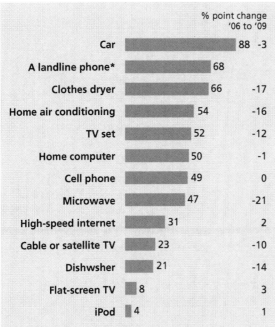

What Americans Need. Percent rating each item as a necessity. Question wording: Do you pretty much think of this as a necessity or pretty much think of this as a luxury you could do without? Pew Research.

Economic recession has a way of teaching us priorities. Since the era of abundance in the 1990s, the television, the most sacrosanct of all luxury items, is now considered a necessity in only 52% of those surveyed – down from 64%.

The media bombards us daily with things that are attractive and appealing. Advertising moguls are paid millions to find new ways of making us want the things they dangle before us. Credit cards make them easy to purchase. It is no wonder that some think there is a giant conspiracy out there, the purpose of which is to prevent anyone from saving anything! I know my mother would see it that way. "It's a game," she used to say. "And it goes like this. You have money in your pocket, and everyone around you is trying to get it out."

Those words still come back to me every time I leave a Best Buy store with some new gadget that I felt sure I could not live another day without. I get that little tingle of conscience they call "buyer's remorse."

Debt versus Savings

America these days is addicted to credit the way drug addicts are hooked on narcotics. The actual number is hard to nail down, but one source recently stated that the United States owes more than $2.5 trillion in consumer debt. Even if it is off a billion or two, that's a lot! How much is a trillion?

• Our standard nine-digit calculator can't display it. It's a one followed by 12 zeros.

- A trillion one-dollar bills, laid end to end, would reach the sun.
- A trillion dollars amounts to $3,333 for each of America's 300,000,000 people.

David Schwartz, a children's book author, says in his book, *How Much Is a Million?*, "One million seconds comes out to be about 11½ days. A billion seconds is 32 years. And a trillion seconds is 32,000 years."

With that in mind, here are a couple of staggering statistics. As of this writing, the United States federal *deficit* stands at $1.7 trillion. The national *debt* stands at over $15 trillion. The debt is incurred when the government spends more than it takes in. It is the debt that creates the operating deficit that resets annually. These deficits are paid for by the government selling interest bearing Treasury securities.

This is where you gulp and swallow hard. *If* the federal government were ever to *default* on its promise to pay periodic interest payments or to repay the debt at maturity, the economy would spin into chaos and collapse. It is the interest on the national debt that gives the shivers to those who track this and understand what it means.

That's why the question is often asked, "Will Medicare and Social Security be around when I retire?" The answer is "yes", if you retire before 2024. The answer is "maybe", if you retire after that. According to the trustees who report on those programs annually, Medicare's trust fund will run dry by 2024, and the Social Security will dry up in 2033. We say "maybe" those programs will still be here because steps will probably be taken to preserve Medicare and Social Security. But it remains to be seen what form those measures will take, and how the face of Medicare and Social Security will change as a result.

Sparse Savings

According to the Employee Benefit Research Institute, about 60% of American workers say their household savings and investments total less than $25,000. According to the book, *The Narcissism Epidemic,* published in 2009, average credit card debt in the United States exceeds $11,000 – triple what it was in 1990. That's just *credit card* debt and doesn't include what we owe on our houses, boats, and cars, etc.

How much are Americans saving for retirement? Not nearly enough. The average American worker spends 94% of disposable income. The EBRI's report breaks down by age group the retirement savings of America as follows:
- Under 35: $6,306
- 35 – 44: $22,460

- 45 – 54: $43,797
- 55 – 64: $69,127
- 65 – 75: $56,212

It's All a Matter of Priorities

I do not recall ever going out to eat as a kid. Even after our belts were a little looser and we no longer ate government cheese, my father and mother were both too conscious of laying a foundation for our family's future to waste money on something as frivolous as ordering from a menu. To this day, regardless of my financial situation, my eyes still go to the right side of the menu first,

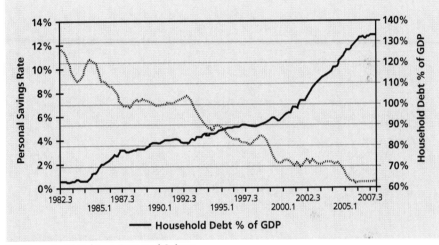

US Household Debt vs. Personal Svings.

where the prices are listed. I can't help it. It is a habit I learned from my frugal parents, who knew the value of a *dime*, and even more so the value of a dollar. Any surplus was to be used as a foundation for our future, not wasted.

Today, when I see young people eating out in a fancy restaurant, I can't help but wonder if they have taken care of the necessities of life first. If not, then they are eating on borrowed money that will eventually have to be paid back by someone. I don't mean to sound like the curmudgeon who resents seeing others experience joy. It just makes me wonder if we are perhaps headed in the wrong direction as a people – a pampered society, not one of industry and thrift. Could it be that retracing our steps back to those taken by an earlier generation might be the best way to move forward to the rich lives we all envision for ourselves?

Summary
Baby Step One: Take a Look Around

Yogi Berra is credited with saying, "You've got to be very careful if you don't know where you're going, because you might not get there." To get to a ridiculously reliable retirement income plan, you first must take stock of where you are. Understand the economic environment around you.

If you are young, start saving now, even if it hurts. Lose the movies and evenings out if you have to, but save at least 10% if not 20% of your income. A dollar saved today and invested properly will be worth five dollars when you need it for retirement. Your parents had more guarantees than you do. Learn this chant, "If it is to be, it's up to me," and say it every time you want to buy something you don't need. Credit card debt is your enemy, not your friend. Get rid of it ASAP. Get a life insurance policy now with a death benefit of at least five times your annual salary while the premiums are low.

If you are in your middle years, take full advantage of any tax deferred retirement plan at work. If your company has a 401(k) and they provide matching funds, contribute the maximum, even if it hurts. If you are self -employed, create your own IRA and pump as much as you can into it. Live within your means. Adjust your needs/wants priorities to provide a foundation for the future.

If you are approaching retirement, recognize that you must change gears from accumulation to preservation. Follow the rule of 100 when it comes to investing. Take your age, subtract it from 100, and that's the amount of money you should have at risk. The rest must be in an absolutely safe place. Take a look around. There are ways for you too to have a retirement income plan that is ridiculously reliable.

Step Two

Understand Your Surroundings

CHAPTER THREE

Beware of Financial Evaporation

*"A big part of financial freedom is having your heart and mind
free from worry about the what-ifs of life."*
- Suze Orman

When it is my turn to tell the bedtime stories in our family, I have a limited, but highly effective arsenal of tales guaranteed to make my daughter's eyelids grow heavy and finally close within 10 minutes. I know nothing of hypnotism, but I am convinced that it is the cadence and the tone with which I read these stories that makes them so sedative. One of Caroline's favorites is *The Little Engine that Could*.

It is the stirring saga of a small, underpowered steam locomotive that bravely volunteered to pull a long train over a high mountain, and could only accomplish the seemingly impossible task by repeating the optimistic chant, "I think I can-I think I can." Sure enough, through hard work and positive thinking, the objective is met, and the little engine emerges a hero. Unfortunately, or fortunately, depending on your point of view, little Caroline usually falls asleep before the part where the little engine proudly chugs into the train yard to the cheers of his railroad pals.

During our accumulation years, while we are still working and saving, we are called upon to haul freight uphill, as it were, in preparing ourselves for retirement. In our younger years, it may be a struggle to chunk away the money we know we ought to save. We are hard wired for having fun. Every cell in our body seems to be thinking of ways to live beyond our means. Then, along comes a family, and our resources seem to be stretched as thin as cheap cellophane. But, like the little engine that could, we give it a go. We chug along. We stick to the program. Then a magic thing happens along the way. Slowly but surely, we get something called momentum. Our capacity to earn becomes greater the more experience we acquire. Our little nest egg begins to grow exponentially – that is – the bigger it gets, the bigger it can get. Because of the miracle of compound interest, what started slowly picks up speed. We keep pressure in the boiler, we keep our eyes focused on our goal and before long, the Law of Inertia begins to work in our favor. Our money is begetting money, which, in turn, begets more money, until we are at last on top of our personal mountain saying, "I knew I could, I knew I could."

Inertia and Compound Interest

Galileo, a 17th century scientist, figured out that it's easier to keep something rolling once you have it rolling than it is to get it rolling in the first place. Sir Isaac Newton came along a few years later and named it the Law of Inertia. A body in motion will tend to remain in motion until it is acted upon by an outside force. It's the same way with money. The first few years of accumulating money are the hardest. After that, if we keep on accumulating and investing wisely, it gets easier. Have you ever heard the saying, "the rich get richer?" Well, they weren't just kidding. It's a natural law of economics that the more we have, the faster it grows, especially when compound interest is involved.

The Power of a Penny

The story is told (fictional, I'm sure) of a job interview where the applicant is offered a job and asked to choose between two pay plans. One compensation plan would pay a straight $1,000 per week. The second plan would pay you a penny per day, doubling every day. That's right…first day on the job nets you a penny. That amount doubles on day two and every day thereafter so that by the end of the first week you have earned a whopping 64 cents. Bad deal, right? Not really. With the penny-doubling-every-day pay plan, you will have earned **over $5 million** by the end of the month! If you are skeptical of the math, just get out your calculator and a calendar and check it. It's true! In the chart below, a penny is doubling each day for 30 days. By the 30th day you have 536,870,912 pennies. That's a cool $5,368,709.12.

1	2	4	8	16	32	64
128	256	512	1,024	2,048	4096	8,192
16,384	32,768	65,546	131,072	262,144	524,288	1,048,576

2,079,152	4,194,304	8,388,608	16,777,286
33,554,432	67,105,864	134,217,728	268,435,456
536,870,912			

A penny doubling every day is, in essence, earning 100% interest paid daily. While that is unrealistic, it does well illustrate the value of momentum when it comes to money…how that even a small amount, over time, can lead to a surprisingly large growth through the miracle of compound interest.

Albert Einstein is often quoted as saying, "Compound interest is the eighth wonder of the world. He who understands it, earns it. He who does not, pays it." Whether the German-born American Physicist actually said that or not is still debated. But it does not negate the truth of the quotation. Compound interest occurs when interest is added to the principal, so that from that moment on, the interest that has been added, also earns interest.

Financial Evaporation

If we are to arrive at a ridiculously reliable retirement income plan, we must keep our eyes peeled for something called financial evaporation – the slow and often imperceptible disappearance of our assets that occurs when we aren't looking, or aren't looking closely enough. Which brings us to the tadpole story.

Summers were long, hot, and sometimes boring in the little milling community in North Carolina where I grew up. If you've ever seen the old black and white reruns of *The Andy Griffith Show*, you have a pretty clear idea of bucolic setting in rural America that comprised my surroundings as a 10-year-old boy. Since my brothers and I did not have much to do, or much to do it with, we invented ways to amuse ourselves. Our favorite play area was a bog near our house where a slow-running creek fed a small swamp. Working like beavers, we dammed up the creek until we had a pond deep enough to swim in.

We boys were intrepid souls. Because we were utterly unaware of them, we were quite unafraid of the dangerous water moccasins that lurked in those waters. A bit further down the food chain were the harmless amphibians with which we shared our aquatic playground. One warm spring day, we discovered in one of the shallow pools near the creek what seemed like millions of little swimmers we would later identify as tadpoles. This was before the internet and the discovery channel, so we had no idea what they were at first. We found some jars and scooped up a few scores of the soon-to-be frogs and took them home. Since our mother did not take too kindly to having them inside the house, we found an old dog food bowl outside and made that their new home, putting it well out of the dog's reach, of course.

"Those aren't fish," my father told us, "those are tadpoles. They will turn into frogs in a few weeks…if they live long enough."

I think he knew something about the attention span of young boys.

"I would advise you to keep them out of the hot sun," he warned.

Over the next few days, we checked on our little swimmers, who at the time seemed very happy. We noticed that they were getting a bit fatter and that some of them had developed little paddles that were the beginnings of frog legs.

We put them in the shade, just like Dad had said. What we did not count on, however, was the shade moving as the sun made its arc across the sky. One morning, after a particularly hot day, we checked on the tadpoles, only to discover that the bowl was bone dry and coated with what looked like small, whip shaped leathery decals stuck to the sides of the bowl. Poor little critters. The heat of the sun had caused the water in the bowl to evaporate, ending any chance our tadpoles had at eventual froghood. Our neighborhood pals who lived next door had better success with their tadpoles. They kept their bowl full of water, and their little tadpoles were still swimming. Overall, I learned the valuable lesson about caring for tadpoles – evaporation happens. In hindsight, we boys should have *repositioned* those tadpoles into a bigger bowl. We should have added water to the bowl. We should have paid more attention.

If we aren't paying attention, the same thing can happen to us in a financial sense. All too often I have seen people build up a nice portfolio that it took decades to acquire. They were counting on these retirement accounts to be there for them when they make their metamorphosis into retirement. Then, evaporation happened. Sizable portions of that reserve disappeared. Was it because they didn't pay enough attention? Did they trust someone else, perhaps a broker, to look after things for them? Did they forget that as they grew older, their risk tolerance would change? Was their ship on autopilot when they should have been tending the wheel? Was their fortune placed in the hands of a financial professional who worked according to some cookie-cutter investing formula that did not take their age into account?

Future Proofing

The best expression I have heard for making sure that evaporation doesn't erode our retirement savings is "**future proofing.**" It reminds me of how we add insulation to a room if we want to temperature proof it so the room remains comfortable during temperature ups and downs. "Future proofing" boils down to something as simple as adhering to one of the oldest rules of investing – the *rule of 100*. Just put a percent sign after your age. That is the amount you should have in a safe place – in the shade – safe from financial evaporation.

Safe does not have to be boring, as we will find out later in this book. What's important is that a safety-minded approach will prevent you from risking money you cannot afford to lose. A competent financial advisor will be able to identify for you, programs that are designed specifically for those approaching retirement – income planning programs that replenish the account each year, regardless of outside forces, such as the stock market and world events.

Had we D'Arruda brothers taken the proactive steps of checking on our tadpoles more frequently and refilling their bowl with creek water more often, our tadpoles would have survived metamorphosis. The "set it and forget it" approach may work well in our early years of investing, simply because time is on our side, but as we approach retirement, we have to be proactive with our accounts if we want them to thrive and grow.

Evaporation takes many forms. It can take the form of unnecessary fees, commissions and needless losses. What's wrong with this statement? "I don't feel bad about my broker losing so much money in my account because everyone else has lost money too." Really? Is that how *you* feel, or is that how you have been programmed to feel? Is the automatic response from your broker one of consolation based on shared experience? When you point out that you pay the same exorbitant fees when your account loses money as you do when it gains, do you receive thorough explanations and solutions? Or do you hear expressions such as:

"Don't feel like the Lone Ranger."

"You're not the only one."

"Everybody's in the same boat."

Don't buy it. Just like those tadpoles that were sensitive to their environment and needed repositioning for their safety, your money needs to be rebalanced and repositioned so that the account won't evaporate from exposure to high risk or exposure to unnecessary fees and commissions.

CHAPTER FOUR

Watch Out For Inflation

"Economic medicine that was previously meted out by the cupful has recently been dispensed by the barrel. These once unthinkable dosages will almost certainly bring on unwelcome after-effects. Their precise nature is anyone's guess, though one likely consequence is an onslaught of inflation."
– Warren Buffett

With 10,000 people retiring every day, we are reminded of the start of a big city marathon. The image of runners clogging the starting line stretches back into seeming infinity, waiting for the signal to start a 26-mile run. Some of them will sail, and some of them will fail. Others will make it, but not without a struggle. But one thing is sure. The ones who succeed, are the ones who know what is in front of them and are prepared for it. The race for success in retirement similarly hinges on us knowing what challenges may confront us and learning how to meet them. When people talk about inflation, you will hear terms like "contained" and "under control" tossed about. That leaves the impression that it is a monster in a cage that could someday escape and wreak havoc on our retirement savings. That's a pretty accurate assumption.

The Frog and Inflation

Financial evaporation is also caused by inflation. The effects of inflation are not sudden and dynamic; they are slow and erosive. If you were to put a frog into a pot of boiling water, the frog would jump out right away. But put the frog in water that is room temperature, slowly turn the heat up, and the frog will allow itself to be cooked without protest. Now, before you sic the animal rights people on me, I have never done this…I have no intention of doing this…and I certainly don't encourage anyone else to do this. I love frogs. I love all amphibians, as a matter of fact. I merely use this example to show the slow, insidious effects of inflation on our wealth.

Why Do We Have Inflation?

If you could lay your hands on a 1913 fifty dollar bill, you would find across the bottom of the bill these words, *"United States of America Fifty Dollars In Gold Coin Payable to the Bearer on Demand."* All paper currency, in fact, used to be backed by pure gold. Over time, however, the dollar was taken off the gold standard. All links with gold were officially severed in 1971. Eventually, the value of paper money was more or less set by a designated agency of the government and measured by a more complicated formula based on the economy in general. The government has the authority to print money, but the more it prints, the less the currency is worth. The less the currency is worth, the fewer goods and services a unit of the currency will buy. Inflation is when prices of goods and services rise, usually followed by a rise in wages.

When all currency was based on gold, there could be no inflation unless new gold reserves were located. As this book is being written, there is a movement underway to return to the gold standard. So far, it has received little traction toward becoming law.

Those who remember the high inflation of the late 1970s and early 1980s can recall when interest rates were in the high teens. Demand raced ahead of supply, and by 1980, the inflation rate had surged as high as 13.5%. By comparison, the inflation rate of 3.5% in 2011 is probably considered downright attractive! But inflation is still a wealth killer. We may tend to take it lightly because it is benign. "Three percent? That's no big deal!" you might say. "That's only three cents on the dollar!"

We have already illustrated the power of a few pennies continually compounded over time in a positive way. Just reverse the process and see the financial evaporation that can result from a few cents. The math does not lie. Just 3%, if not adjusted for, can seriously erode our financial independence in retirement. Just ask those who have been retired for 20 or 30 years if inflation has had any impact on the purchasing power of their fixed incomes.

A Penny Saved…

One way to counteract inflation evaporation is through thrift. If inflation is at 3%, then save 3%. As a financial advisor, I love the concept of saving money. Benjamin Franklin is one of my personal heroes. He is the one who coined the timeless proverb, "A penny saved is a penny earned." If prices are outrageous, wait for a sale. Beat the system by clipping coupons. If you have a dollar-off coupon for something you truly need, it's jackpot time! However, beware of shopping just for shopping's sake. That just defeats the purpose.

Saving isn't always saving. One way *not* to fight inflation is to stockpile your money into certificates of deposit that are paying 1% or 2% interest when inflation is around 4%. Not only do you have a net loss of the difference, but if you add in the interest you could have earned with a more sensible, and still safe, investment, then you are taking two giant steps backward. Losing money safely is still losing money. Competent financial advisors will be able to point you toward defined accounts that have contractually guaranteed growth that will still pay you more than the inflation rate. A desirable feature of these accounts is the ability to move from one interest generating environment to another inside the product.

Learning from Mistakes

One financial planner is reported to have told his clients following the 2008 market crash, "You have to remember, all boats sink some in a falling tide." The couple had just gotten the news that 40% of their life savings had been virtually wiped out overnight. Money counted on for retirement was now blowing in the wind like a dandelion poof. The reverse side of the axiom was then uttered, "And when the tide rises, all boats rise with it."

Please keep in mind that these folks were on the verge of retirement. They could not afford the loss of that much of their life savings at so critical a time in their lives. That one-liner about tides and boats is both insensitive and untruthful. It is tantamount to a surgeon losing a patient on the operating table, and shrugging to the grieving family, "Well, you win some, and you lose some."

I am not in the medical field, so I cannot speak to what should and shouldn't be done in the operating room. But as a trained financial planner, I can tell you that the advisor could have taken measures that would have prevented the couple's loss.

I live two hours from the Atlantic Ocean, and I know a little about boats and tides. The falling/rising tide illustration the broker used to explain away the sudden loss of the couple's money is clever, but it just doesn't wash. It suggests that we should just accept the rising and falling of an economic tide as something that occurs every few hours and can do no lasting harm. It is as if to say, "Oh sure, you lose a little when the tide goes out; but you gain it all back when the tide comes back in." That wasn't the case here. The loss experienced by these people was not usual and customary. It was devastating and preventable. Fitting that kind of loss into a falling/rising tide scenario would require the ocean to leave the harbor entirely, expose the ocean bed for miles, and then come back in at the rate of a few feet per day.

At the coast, there are boatyards that are used as dry docks when a hurricane threatens to come ashore. These areas are largely empty of boats until a major storm is predicted. Until then, boat owners leave their vessels bobbing peacefully in the harbors and marinas for convenience. However, once the storm surge is predicted, the dry docks fill up fast. Huge cranes hoist heavy boats out of the water and place them on blocks. Forklifts move smaller boats to warehouses where they are stored indoors until the storm passes. Owners who fail to take such precautions may have their boats severely damaged by the storm, or perhaps lose their boats altogether – all because of either inattention or poor decision making. So it's not true that what happens to one boat has to happen to them all. Likewise, money can be protected from loss by making the right decisions as to its placement and use.

There is an old proverb that makes a great deal of sense. "Smart people learn from their mistakes; geniuses learn from the mistakes of others." Wise financial planners know how to position the assets of those nearing retirement so that they do not experience unacceptable losses. To knowledgeable and competent financial advisors who are trained in retirement planning, the very idea of you losing your retirement savings because of the volatility of the stock market is patently unacceptable.

Staying Above "C" Level

My father, who was a college professor, was an exacting man when it came to the academic performance of his children.

"You want to know why people drown?" he used to say. "Because they didn't stay above 'C' level."

If any of the D'Arruda boys came into the house with a "C" on their report card, it was not going to be a pleasant evening. I had two brothers - one was two years younger and the other was four years younger than I. On the rare occasions when one of us did bring home a "C", we quickly learned that there were no excuses that would fly. We knew never to use the excuse, "But everyone else got a 'C', too." There were a string of reasons my father used to invalidate that theory. We were quickly informed it was ridiculous to think that our test results and grades were inevitably bound to equal those of our schoolmates. My favorite line of his was what I later dubbed the "lemming rebuttal." Lemmings have had the reputation for going off cliffs in droves ever since they were portrayed doing so in the 1955 Disney film, *White Wilderness.*

"Is your last name Lemming?" he would ask. "If everybody else jumped off a cliff, would you do it too?" The point did sink in that just because everyone makes a mistake, that doesn't condemn you to imitating it. There was no definition for it in those days, but today, we call it "tough love." My father was exacting because his standards for us were high. I learned to simply study my lessons and do my homework. That way, I was never surprised by a pop quiz or a hard test. I knew the material going in. Study hard and do your work, and the grades will take care of themselves.

Being caught on the wrong end of a stock market downturn simply means that we were not proactive enough with the handling of our monetary affairs. There's no way of getting around the pure and simple truth that we made a poor decision, even if it was deciding not to decide. Being proactive in a financial sense simply means positioning yourself in such a way that you can't be hurt. The secret of success in this regard involves the dividing of our money into different strategies, or different buckets, so that in case we happen to make a bad decision, it only affects some of the money. The rest of the money is invested where it is safe from loss, so we stay well above "C" level.

Summary
Baby Step Two: Understand Your Surroundings

We all make decisions without all the facts from time to time. But some people spend more time studying a restaurant menu before a meal than they do paying attention to what their money is doing. Be proactive. Take Charge. If you are nearing retirement, or are in retirement, use the rule of 100 to determine your risk tolerance. Put a percent sign after your age and keep that much of your assets where your principle cannot be lost.

Remember the tadpoles. Neglect and inattention is what truly did them in. The hot sun and subsequent evaporation were the result of not paying enough attention. Financial evaporation can take place when your assets are placed in strategies that are either too risky or come with exorbitant and unnecessary fees. Examine your monthly, quarterly or annual account statements. Watch for signs of evaporation.If you see something that gives you pause, then get a second opinion from a qualified financial advisor who is sensitive to your age and your proximity to retirement.

When you are taking aim on your retirement goal, account for inflation. Hopefully it won't spiral again like it did in the late 1970s and early 1980s – but you never know. Even if it is "under control", it is still a slow creeper that can slowly choke your wealth.

Get involved with your money. Don't just follow the crowd when it comes to investing. Learn from the mistakes of other people. Get a second opinion if you don't understand your account statements. If you are nearing retirement, or are in retirement, and you are losing money, get a second opinion. What could it hurt?

Step Three

Looking for Support

CHAPTER FIVE

Why You Can't Rely Just on Social Security

*"To every American out there on Social Security,
to every American supporting that system today,
and to everyone counting on it when they retire,
we made a promise to you, and we are going to keep it."*
- George H.W. Bush, January 31, 1990

To depend on Social Security to get you through retirement is chancy at best, gambling at worst. Yet the latest statistics reveal that 35% of Americans will have only their Social Security checks to rely on when they retire. In 2010, the average monthly payout received by a Social Security beneficiary amounted to a paltry $1,094. If you can live on that, then good for you. But most people I know can't. But, then again, Social Security was never intended to be a retirement income fund. When the Social Security Act was signed into law by President Franklin D. Roosevelt in 1935, he told the American public, "We can never insure one-hundred percent of the population against one-hundred percent of the hazards and vicissitudes of life." FDR probably did not know just how right his words would turn out to be.

Social Security was intended to be a pay-as-you-go trust fund but in 2011, administration trustees projected that the system would be broke by 2037. The reason is simple. The trust is paying out billions more each year in retirement, disability and survivor benefits than it takes in. That can't last. Either dramatic changes will be made in the system, or it will disappear. If the system is rescued, as likely it will be, it will not look the same for the next generation of retirees.

Since the system is that unpredictable and unreliable, the best thing future generations can do is forget about Social Security as being anything but a nice little sidebar to the money they personally arrange for in their older years. Create your own retirement savings/income account.

What Does Retirement Look Like To You?

If you close your eyes and I say the word "retirement", what mental picture appears in that little cartoon thought bubble over your head? It is going to be a different picture for each person. There was a time when most Americans had the stereotypical view of retirement that involved a rocking chair on the porch and such sedentary activities as whittling for the men and knitting for the women. If that is still your view of retirement, then perhaps you will be able to get by with less, but no one truly wants that kind of retirement today. For one thing, a life that is void of interesting activity leads to more health issues and a shorter lifespan. Our goals and aspirations are what keep us going.

Most grandparents I talk to tell me that they just love the job.

"I did my duty as a father," said one man. "I was careful not to spoil my kids. It's a different story with my grandchildren. I just enjoy them."

He went on to explain that it gives him pleasure to be generous with them. He said he never misses a birthday and loves to see their eyes light up when they open their presents.

"They never forget that kind of thing," he said.

No one I know of would like to have such limited resources in retirement that they would feel embarrassed to go to their grandchildren's birthday party. Most would rather to be in a position to help them with their education if necessary, or give them help in starting their own families some day.

In retirement, every day is a weekend. I don't know about you, but I spend much more money on the weekend than I do on weekdays. When you visualize retirement, you may intend to be thrifty and live within your means. But saying it to yourself and doing it are two different things.

Know Your Number

I am always amused when I see the television commercial that shows people walking down the street with numbers under their arms. The six and seven-figure numbers represent the amount they need to have saved in order to safely retire. Then there is the guy trimming his hedges who has no clue what he needs to have saved up before he retires. His number is "Gazillion." The point of the commercial, of course, is that you need to *plan* for retirement.

Most people retire by a certain age, the most popular being 65. Like the "seeker" used to call out in the childhood game hide and seek, "Ready or not; here I come!" Similarly, as with the hedge clipper with his "Gazillion," many just aim to amass as much as they can and then call it a day.

The more intelligent approach, however, is to get out the calculator and figure up how much you need to live on for the rest of your live. Consult with a competent financial advisor who specializes in income planning. The financial professional will be able to plug in your answer and back into your "magic number," or how much you will need to save.

Here is an exercise that may help. Get a legal pad and create three columns with headings, "Expenses," "Now" and "Retired" at the top. On the left side of the page, list all your expenses by categories and enter the dollar amounts across

EXPENSES	NOW	RETIRED
Housing		
Utilities		
Food		
Clothing		
Transportation		
Insurance		
Travel		
Medical Care		
Gifts		
TOTAL		
INCOME		
Salary		
Pension		
Investments		
Social Security		
TOTAL		

the page where they apply. Under the "Now" Column, for example, you may have an expense that you won't have when you are retired. But, if you plan to travel in retirement, that expense will show up under the "Retired" heading. Be as specific as possible with your expenses. Of course, you will list expenses such as food, clothing and transportation. But don't forget to include such items as insurance, taxes, gifts and utilities. Next, at the bottom of that sheet, list your sources of income now and during retirement. Here is where you may wish to obtain the services of a competent retirement income specialist to determine how to make the most out of your resources and figure out if you have saved enough to retire.

This kind of worksheet will give you a financial snapshot that will let you know if you are ready to retire.

Example: With no mortgage payment, occasional dining out and two trips a year, I think I could enjoy retirement at around $60,000 per year. If I can squeeze that amount out of my savings, I'm there!

Remember, if your goal is to have a retirement income that is *guaranteed to last the rest of your life*, then tell your financial professional that. Make it clear that you are not interested in projections or prognostications. You want guarantees that make it clear in writing what you can expect to receive, either in your mailbox or deposited into your checking account, every month, from the day you retire until the day you die. If that is what you want, and the answer doesn't conform to it, then by all means, obtain a second opinion.

Pleasant Surprise

Over the years, I have enjoyed helping people from all backgrounds and walks of life find their number. One observation I have made is that everyone has a different number, and everyone feels differently about their number. For some, no number, no matter how large, would ever be enough. For others, they are pleasantly surprised and relieved when they learn it.

One such case presented itself to me a few years ago. A woman came to my office after having just had the news delivered to her that she was no longer needed at her place of employment. She was 61 and had been with this firm for almost 20 years. The company was on shaky ground financially, and massive layoffs resulted. Jobs were scarce. She wondered what kind of work she could find at her age.

As I listened to her lay out her financial picture, I discovered that she had been a careful saver. Her modest home was paid for. She was debt free. She had contributed the maximum amount to a 401(k) at work and her company had provided a generous match. She had almost $300,000 in savings. With that amount, plus her small pension and her social security check, she could have a comfortable monthly income that would last her the rest of her life. She went from tears of despair to tears of joy. She had no idea that she was in a position to safely retire.

CHAPTER SIX

The Case of the Disappearing Pension

"A corporation's responsibility is to the shareholders,
not its retirees and employees. Companies are doing everything
they can to get rid of pension plans, and they will succeed."
- Ben Stein

There was a time in America when you would work for a company for 30 or 40 years, knowing that in the future you could retire with a defined benefit pension plan. It would be waiting for you at the end of the trail, just like a faithful retirement angel, guaranteeing you and your spouse at least 75% of your old salary for the rest of your lives. You were set.

Somewhere in the 1980's those plans started to cough and gasp and by the end of the 1990s, they were almost extinct, replaced by plans that called for employees to save on their own through a company sponsored plan. The defined *benefit* plan had given way to the defined *contribution* plan.

Defined benefits means just what it says. When you reach that age where it's time to collect your pension, your benefit is defined. It is clearly spelled out and guaranteed in writing, typically good for life, for both you and your spouse.

Defined contribution means just what it says. Employees contribute to a plan whereby the amount contributed is specified, usually tax deferred, and typically invested until retirement. When the employee retires, he or she can take benefits. The benefits are usually not defined, because that all depends on how the investments performed over the years.

The Endangered Pension

Just where the idea came into the heads of Americans that they were entitled to a pot of gold at the end of the rainbow is not clear. At the end of World War II, there was a certain euphoria that existed. America had just defeated her enemies in war and now was emerging as the great golden empire. The depression was over and hard times were replaced by happy days. The good life could be had by the ordinary working man. Just get on with a big company with a good pension and, as long as you put in your years of service with them, you could live the American dream.

The first inkling that pensions may not be able to live up to the commitments made to workers by big business was probably when the Studebaker company went bust in 1963. They were the first major automaker to default on pensions. In 1974, congress passed the Employee Retirement Income Security Act (ERISA), which held corporations accountable for pension trust funds and provided accounting standards that they all were required to meet. Accountants were hired and audits were performed. If it was determined that if a pension fund's liabilities (promises to workers) exceeded its assets, then the deficit could negatively affect the company's value on the market. Pension fund managers that had at first been conservative with pension plan investments eventually gave way to the lure of the lucrative stock market during the boom years of the 1990s. In fact, during those days, many pension plans were overstuffed with assets. Companies could count the pension fund surplus as part of their earnings, and this hiked up the value of those companies measurably.

Then came the market correction of the 2000s. Returns dwindled, and pension plans took a beating. One after another, pension plans began faltering, and corporations began deciding that these burdensome retirement plans were no longer viable.

General Motors, which was forced to declare bankruptcy in 2009, is probably the best example of how the underfunding of pensions can force a large corporation to change from defined benefit plans to defined contribution plans. In its June 6, 2009 issue, USA *Today* reported that the giant auto maker's pension plan was underfunded by $20 billion.

Thanks to a government bailout, GM recovered and reported an $8 billion net profit in 2011. But according to the New York Times of February 15, 2012, the GM pension plan was not to be so blessed. Despite the company's comeback, the *Times* reported that pension plan was still underfunded by $8.7 billion. As a result, starting in October of 2012, GM's 19,000 salaried workers who have been covered by GM's pension plan, will be shifted to a 401(k)-type plan. GM had already stopped putting new salaried employees into the pension plan in 2001.

Sadly, a number of companies have been turning to bankruptcy as a way out of burdensome pension obligations. Strategic bankruptcies are still headline news, especially with large corporations like Delta Airlines, but the news is no longer shocking. Only about 20% of today's workers are covered in defined benefit programs. Analysts predict that in the next decade, it will diminish to zero. Of great concern to many, is the fact that some government pension plans, once thought to be above the fray, bear even higher underfunded liabilities than those in the private sector. Towns and municipalities are now forced to choose between keeping their pension promises and providing basic services such as education and road repair.

Create Your Own Pension

If you have a pension, especially one with the guarantees described earlier in the chapter, then consider yourself one of the fortunate few. But for everyone else, let's face it, we're going to have to create our own pensions. Naturally, the younger you are the better. But, if you wait until later in life, it's still not too late to start a personal pension plan. Make sure you understand what you are doing, of course. There are many upsides to having a personal pension plan as opposed to company sponsored plans. One upside is that you do not have to depend on anyone else. You are not at the mercy of the big company any longer. If you don't like the environment in which you work, you can pick up and leave and take your pension with you. It's yours. You control it. You make the rules.

"Mama may have,
Papa may have.
But God bless the child
That's got his own"

*- First recorded by blues singer Billie Holliday in
1939. Lyrics by Junior Giscombe and Bob Carter.*

CHAPTER SEVEN

401(k)s – A Good News, Bad News Story

"The trouble with retirement is that you never get a day off."
- Abe Lemons

When President Jimmy Carter signed into law the United States Revenue Act of 1978, he probably had no idea that he was changing America's retirement landscape forever. The legislation contained a little noticed (at the time) section 401, paragraph (k) that permitted American workers to save money for retirement and lower their taxes at the same time.

The new law was music to the ears of Ted Benna, a benefits consultant from Philadelphia, who seized upon the language of section 401, paragraph (k) right away. Benna was somewhat of a retirement plan visionary. The wording of the law allowed for bonuses if saved for retirement, to be tax deferred. In other words, if you set the money aside and did not touch it until you retired, you would not pay taxes on the money until you retired. It was Benna who saw that the new rule could also be applied to regular wages, allowing them to receive tax deferment if saved for retirement. Benna had, in fact, been working on a plan that would allow employers to match employee contributions and reap a corporate tax deduction in the process. He submitted the plan to the Internal Revenue Service, which officially approved it in the Spring of 1981, giving birth to the 401(k) defined contribution plan. Despite its somewhat cryptic name, within a decade, the 401(k) would be quickly on its way to eventually replacing defined benefit pension plans across the country.

Good News

There are many facets to the 401(k). One attractive characteristic of these types of savings/investment programs is that the money you put into it is tax deferred as it grows. In other words, you don't pay tax on the money until you take it out. Over time, compound savings, without any reduction for taxes, equals quite a financial advantage over savings and investment programs that are not tax deferred.

Many companies give participants a wide variety of investment options. These choices are designed to help you know your risk tolerance and invest accordingly. On one end of the spectrum will be growth funds, considered to be somewhat risky by many investors, while at the other end of the spectrum will be money market funds, considered the same as cash in the bank. If you make the right choices, then your investments do quite well, especially if you allow the principle of dollar cost averaging to work for you.

If you have a 401(k), it is important that you get the most out of it. If your employer offers matching funds, it usually means that the only way to get a contribution from the company is to make a contribution yourself. Some employers have generous matching programs while others have meager ones. Some employers do not match at all. Two of the most common matching programs go as follows:

50% match up to the first 6% – This means that for every dollar you put into your retirement plan, your employer will place 50 cents into the plan. There is a limit of 6% of your gross salary per year that the employer will match. Someone with a $50,000 salary, for example, who contributes at least 6% to his/her 401(k) plan, will receive a matching contribution from the employer of $1,500.

Dollar for dollar match up to 5% - This means that for every dollar you put in your 401(k) plan, the company will also put in a dollar. Once you reach a total of 5% of your gross pay contributed for the year, your employer won't add any more dollars to your account until the next calendar year.

I would advise anyone to take advantage of a company match of any description. It's free money, and that is always a good idea. Keep in mind that there are many variations on this theme. For example, your company's contributions may be based on a vesting schedule. In other words, the money's there, but you have to stay with the firm long enough, say 20 years or so, to get the full amount.

Bad News

A lot of people I talk to in the financial industry have unpleasant things to

say about the 401(k). Some call it the biggest rip-off in history. That may be a little harsh, but few dispute the charge that 401(k)s were set up for the purpose of advancing the cause of mutual funds, which is where most of the money from such programs is invested.

One negative aspect to 401(k)s is hidden fees. Fees associated with 401(k)s should be transparently disclosed on the statements provided to employees and many times they are not. Many of these fees are referred to in the financial community as "inner fees" or "production fees." They are sometimes difficult to parse out from the other information that appears on the statement. They sometimes take the form of "management fees," which are another word for sales commissions. These are fees that you pay out of your paycheck, but likely didn't knowingly agree to.

In most cases, employers contract with a fund manager to come into the workplace and enroll employees into the program. These folks are the ones who should, but often do not, provide full disclosure on these fees and commissions.

On the list of 401(k) drawbacks is possible market loss. When untrained investors see their accounts lose money, they sometimes make investment decisions emotionally. They see the market ebb and flow and watch their money fall and surge with it. To some, this is maddening, especially when they are in the "red zone" – within 10 years of retirement. They either change their allocations based on fear, or attempt to time the market by moving in and out of mutual funds to their disadvantage. In my opinion, the best way to manage a 401(k) where you are given decision-making power is to use a manager. Allow a trained professional to invest your money based on your age, your risk tolerance levels and according to what your goals are for the future.

There should be more disclosure than there currently is when it comes to fees in 401(k) programs. And employees still have too few investment options. But the most egregious flaw in 401(k) programs is the lack of a guaranteed lifetime income. Employees should know exactly, to the penny, what they can expect to receive in the way of income when they retire. What good is it to save all your life, only to retire with a lump sum that may not last throughout your lifetime?

I applaud those financial planners who recommend tax-free rollovers that, upon retirement, move the money from the 401(k) into an account that better fits what retirement is all about. If set up properly, this account can not only continue providing growth for the assets within the fund, but also provide a guaranteed income that cannot be outlived, in contract form. Many of these contracts can be structured to care for both the one retiree and his or her spouse. Sound familiar? Sound like the defined benefit pension plans of old? Yes, it does. But it could be done within the framework of the current 401(k) programs and it would be a win-win for all concerned.

Comparison of Roth 401(k), Roth IRA, and Traditional 401(k) Retirement Accounts

Characteristic	Designated Roth 401(k) Account	Roth IRA	Traditional, Pre-Tax 401(k) Account
Contributions	Designated Roth employee elective contributions are made with **after-tax dollars**.	Roth IRA contributions are made with **after-tax dollars**.	Traditional, pre-tax employee elective contributions are made with **before-tax dollars**.
Income Limits	No income limitation to participate.	Income limits: married $179,000/ single $122,000 modified AGI for 2011	No income limitation to participate.
Maximum Elective Contribution	*Aggregate** employee elective contributions limited to $16,500 in 2011 ($22,000 for employees 50 or over).	Same aggregate* limited to $5,000 in 2011 ($6,000 for employees 50 or over).	Contribution limit as Designated Roth 401(k) Account.
Taxation of Withdrawals	Withdrawals of contributions and earnings are **not** taxed provided it's a **qualified distribution** – the account is held for at least 5 years and made: • On account of disability, • On or after death, or • On or after attainment of age 59½.	Same as Designated Roth 401(k) Account and can have a qualified distribution for a first time home purchase.	Withdrawals of contributions and earnings **are** subject to Federal and most State income taxes.
Required Distributions	Distributions must begin no later than age 70½, unless still working and not a 5% owner.	No requirement to start taking distributions while owner is alive.	Same as Designated Roth 401(k) Account.

* This limitation is by individual, rather than by plan. Although permissible to split the annual employee elective contribution between designated Roth contributions and traditional, pre-tax contributions, the combination cannot exceed the deferral limit - $17,000/$22,500 (for 2012).

Information obtained from the Internal Revenue Service, www.IRS.gov/retirement

Roth 401(k)s?

A few companies now are allowing employees to contribute to a Roth 401(k). That provision was approved by congress in 2006. If the company offers this type of plan, employees have the option of amending their plan document to elect ROTH type tax treatment. They can do this for either a portion, or for all of their retirement plan contributions.

Under the Roth 401(k), employees can decide to contribute funds on a post-tax elective deferral basis, in addition to, or instead of, pre-tax elective deferrals under their traditional 401(k) plans. Employers are permitted to make matching contributions on employees' designated Roth contributions.

In general, the difference between a Roth 401(k) and a traditional 401(k) is that the Roth version is funded with **after-tax** dollars while the traditional 401(k) is funded with **pre-tax** dollars. After-tax dollars represent money for which taxes are paid in the current year, and pre-tax dollars are those that do not represent federal taxable income in the current year. Typically, the earnings on Roth contributions will be tax free as long as the distribution is made at least 5 years after the first Roth contribution and the attainment of age 59 and one half, unless an exception applies.

A Roth 401(k) plan will probably be most advantageous to those who might otherwise choose a Roth IRA, for example, younger workers who are currently taxed in a lower tax bracket, but expect to be taxed in a higher bracket upon reaching retirement age. Also, higher-income workers who wish to save the maximum amount allowed may favor the Roth 401(k) because it effectively allows greater real contributions, as post-tax dollars are more valuable than pre-tax dollars.

Tax the Seed or Tax the Harvest

To understand the advantages of a Roth 401(k) over the traditional 401(k), imagine that you are a farmer and it's planting time on the farm. You are standing there with your bag of seed, ready to sow your crop, when along comes Mr. Taxman. He politely takes off his top hat – the red, white and blue one with the stars on it, introduces himself and clears his throat.

"Mr. Farmer," he says to you. "I'm going to give you a choice. Either you can pay me tax right now on that little bag of seed you have in your hand, I will consider it a done deal, and I will go away forever and leave you alone, OR...you can pay me no tax today, whatsoever, on the seed, but I will come back every year and tax you on the harvest."

"Let me get this straight," you say. "If I pay the taxes on the seed today, I'm done with it forever?"

"That's right," says the taxman.

"But you will let me slide on paying the tax on the seed today, if I agree to pay you tax on the harvest forever and ever as long as a crop comes in?"

"That's right," says Mr. Taxman. "So what's it going to be?"

It's a no-brainer, isn't it? You will choose to pay the tax on the seed. Otherwise – let's say it is corn seed. Each year, when the ears of corn are ripe, Uncle Sam comes by and taxes you on each and every ear of corn you pull off, and repeats the process for years.

It's that way with Roth 401(k)s. You pay the tax going in, but never pay taxes again on either that money or the amount by which the account grows. So since Roth 401(k)s are clearly more advantageous to the long term saver/investor, why aren't more companies offering Roth 401(k)s to their employees? Good question. The excuse heard most often is that it would require more administrative help. I tend to doubt that is the real reason. I believe it is a lack of public awareness. Not many employees understand the benefits of such a plan, if they even know that it is available to them. Once enough people in the American workplace become aware, however, they will ask about it, and companies will feel the pressure to keep up with the times. After all, the reason why companies provide retirement programs to begin with, is to attract loyal, competent employees who will stay with them for decades.

Summary
Baby Step Three: Looking for Support

Social Security alone is not going to have enough horsepower to see you through your retirement years, but you probably already knew that. View your Social Security as a nice little side fund and create your own retirement by spending less and saving as much as possible. Even the trustees of the system acknowledge that, without dramatic changes, the Social Security System, as we know it, will not be around by the year 2030. It will likely get a face lift but one that may make it unrecognizable to your children.

If you have one of the rare traditional pensions that guarantee you a lifetime payout after you retire, then consider yourself fortunate. They are on their way out.

If you are young, and you work for a company that offers a 401(k) plan, be regular in your contributions. Dollar cost averaging will see you through. If your employer offers a company match, take full advantage of it. That's free money. If you are approaching retirement, be careful not to take on too much risk. You are ready to retire. You will need that money.

If you aren't sure how much you should have at risk, follow the rule of 100. Put a percent sign after your age and that is the percentage of your money that you should have absolutely safe from loss.

If you don't understand the statements you get from your retirement accounts, then ask questions until you do. If the answers don't sound right, or if you have lost ground in your savings, get a second opinion and find out why. Knowledge and education are your two best friends when it comes to building a ridiculously reliable retirement income plan.

Step Four

Making Your Own Way

CHAPTER EIGHT

Creating a Lifetime Income Strategy

*"Retirement is like a long vacation in Las Vegas.
The goal is to enjoy it the fullest, but not so fully that you
run out of money."* – Anonymous

Hosting a radio talk show and taking calls from listeners with questions about money has taught me to listen more carefully for the question behind the question. For instance, a caller will ask a question such as, "Am I making a mistake to retire when I turn 62, or should I wait until I'm 65?"

What's really going through the caller's mind is, "I'm afraid I may run out of money. I have no guarantee. My money is in a retirement account that is tied to the stock market. What will happen to me if it takes another nosedive?"

When it comes to mapping out a financial future, many don't seem to know exactly and specifically where they are going. In general terms, they may know what they want. They want freedom, independence, and leisure time. But when you ask them to color in the details and explain **exactly how much** income they expect to have coming in each month during their retirement, and exactly where that money will come from, they can't tell you. And yet, if asked, "Would you like to have a guaranteed lifetime income in retirement?" The resounding reply from most people would be "Yes!"

From where I watch the world, one of the most critical topics that needs discussing, and yet one of the most ignored by most financial professionals, is how to create a lifetime income strategy. This is partly the result of uneducated consumers who are not aware that such strategies exist. Could this lack of awareness also be because many financial professionals are button pushers and order takers instead of problem solvers? I think so.

The Water Wheel of Money

What's the waterwheel of money? When colonists first settled the area of North Carolina where I live, they would look for an area where water ran quickly downhill and build a water-powered grist mill. Some of these mills still exist and a few are even still functioning. The early settlers knew that if they were to eat all year long, they would need to have some means by which to grind the corn and wheat into meal and flour so they could make bread. If you have ever seen one of these mills in action, you will see how the natural force of gravity, combined with the motion of running water, serves to create the closest thing to a perpetual motion machine there is. As long as the water keeps flowing, the wheel will continue to turn, powering the gears and cogs of the millworks.

In areas of the country where streams were slower moving, the colonists became engineers, constructing dams and creating artificial waterfalls.

Financial engineers accomplish the same thing when they put in place a mechanism for creating a continuous flow of income from assets that we have accumulated. Financial cruise control occurs when we can just sit back, relax, and watch that water wheel of money turn. We have created it for that purpose. Now it can continue to generate for us a lifetime income that will be there as long as we need it. With the proper planning, we can adjust our financial landscape so that it provides us with a reliable, guaranteed lifetime income.

That image of water cascading over a water wheel puts us in mind of how a lifetime income strategy might work. It's continuous, dependable and self-attending. We don't want to have sleepless nights worrying about how our income in retirement may be threatened by market forces or world events. Those settlers knew that as long as water continued to roll downhill, they would have bread on their tables. We want that kind of peace of mind.

Creating Income Buckets

The mechanics of creating your perpetual money water wheel can well be illustrated by picturing a row of five buckets, each with a different purpose.

Bucket #1 Immediate Income – This bucket represents money that starts in the first year of retirement and continues for the next five years. We are going to put a spigot on the bottom of this bucket that will allow for a steady flow of money for five years. How much do we put in this bucket? That will depend on your chosen lifestyle and your asset level. Here's where a little budgeting and planning needs to be done. You and your financial advisor will establish a budget that's right for you. Then, this bucketful of money will be put in a position where it will be safe from loss, grow at a reasonable rate and provide income for the next five years.

The assets we place in this bucket could take many forms as long as they perform, they meet the criteria of being reliable and they are there for five years. We could use a series of CDs, for example, and stagger the maturity dates. When we exhaust one, we tap into another, all the while letting the money accrue interest as we go.

We could use a combination of CDs and bonds. Or we could use an immediate annuity. Everybody's circumstances are different and exactly which vehicle we use for this five-year income bucket will depend on those circumstances.

Bucket #2 Years Six through Ten - Another five year bucket will now generate the income while the bulk of your assets continues to grow as much as safely possible. As with the first bucket, there are a number of savings/investment vehicles we might use here, all based on individual circumstances.

Bucket #3 Lifetime Income – While our first two buckets have been performing the dual task of providing income and interest, the money bucket #3 has been waiting until year ten to do what we put it here for – generate a lifetime income. Here is where we scan the shelves of all the retirement programs out there for the best guarantees. We will always have an emergency fund if we need it, but it is this block of money that we will look to for long term security and as much growth as safely possible. In today's financial world, there are many products available to retirees that will contractually promise compounded growth *for that income* at 5, 6, or 7% per year. This allows us the ability to look forward into the future and know what awaits us. If you take the right steps, it's almost like having a financial crystal ball.

Bucket #4 Emergency Money – While your other buckets are working for you, either providing income or earning interest, this bucket is kept for emergencies that may present themselves. None of your money should be lazy, so this money will earn interest until you need it. But it must be fully liquid, (money you can put your hands on when you need it without filling out any paper more complicated than a check). How much you keep in it is up to you. As previously mentioned, all circumstances are different. If you are the type of individual who is cautious by nature, you may have a tendency to stuff too much money in this account. Don't worry. You are always able to pull money from your other buckets if absolutely necessary. They may not be quite as liquid, however. The characteristics of this bucket dictate that the money is at your fingertips and available at a moment's notice.

Bucket #5 Extra Money – Now that all of your needs have been accounted for, both current and future, the rest of your assets go into this bucket. You may use it any way you wish. You may wish to blow it on travel. You may wish to use it to provide a legacy for your children or grandchildren. Do you enjoy having some of your assets at risk in the stock market? Then go for it. Risk is not so much a concern here because you are certain of an income that you cannot outlive. The market is a turbulent place. But you are psychologically better able to deal with its ups and downs if you aren't so worried about the downticks interfering with your lifestyle. It is still a good idea to follow the rule of 100 (a percent sign after your age tells you how much money you should have completely safe). But now you may be more creative with your investments, if you desire.

Core Money and Explore Money

Call your safe money your "core" money, because it is at the very center of what propels your water wheel/income mill. Call your other money your "explore" money, because you can use it to explore investments that may return better than average rates of return for you in your golden years. Don't forget to congratulate yourself. You have placed your assets in what is called an "advance and protect" strategy. In other words, you are always going forward while protecting what you have.

Don't Fumble Now

In football, the red zone refers to the last 20 yards before the end zone on the football field. When you are that close to the goal line, everything changes. Offenses have special plays to adapt for a shorter playing field. The cardinal rule for everyone who touches the ball in the red zone is, whatever you do, don't turn the ball over. Many a game has been decided by a fumble just when the prize is within reach of the team with the ball.

If you watch football, maybe you have seen the ball carrier try to stretch for that extra yard by holding the ball in one hand and extending that arm as far as he can. Then a defensive player swats it free and the drive is over. Good coaches tell their players to keep the ball safely tucked away under the arm closest to the sideline and hold it with two hands.

Likewise, if you are in the retirement red zone – that is just retired or within ten years of retirement – now is no time to fumble the ball by playing fast and loose with your savings. You may reason that risk is required so as to make up for lost time. But the "advance and protect" strategy needs to be employed here. Keep your money tucked away safely. Advance the ball, to be sure! But risk only what you can afford to lose. The ball is your retirement income. You simply cannot be risky with that money, not at this stage of the game.

CHAPTER NINE

Do You Need an Annuity Rescue?

"Time is nature's way of keeping everything from happening at once." – Woody Allen

A s a broadcaster, I have learned that people want things simple. However, as a financial advisor, I have learned that simple is not always easy when it comes to money matters. If you make it too simple, you gloss over important facts that need to be understood. Over the years, I'm sure that I have irritated some folks who came to me for advice because I insisted that they understood the details of a document they were signing, or by making doubly sure that they fully understood a financial instrument into which they were placing their assets. But I believe fine print is meant to be read. In fact, when the type gets tiny, that's when I read more carefully than ever before. When it comes to money, there are no stupid questions. They all deserve answers. That is especially true when large amounts of money, perhaps your life's savings, are on the line.

In the financial world today, too many people have fallen for the enticement of a glossy brochure and put their money into financial vehicles that they didn't understand, only to have it come back to bite them. Annuities can be useful tools in helping people reach their financial goals. But there is no one-size-fits-all annuity. They are complex financial instruments with several moving parts.

What Is an Annuity?
An annuity is merely a contract offered by an insurance company that is

similar to a CD with a bank. But because they are offered by insurance companies, and because insurance companies have actuaries, annuities can offer the extra feature of a "guaranteed lifetime income," which is something banks can't do. But in most other respects, especially with fixed annuities, they behave in a similar manner. They pay interest, and like CDs owners, annuity owners pay penalties for early withdrawal.

All annuities grow tax-deferred, which means that the earnings inside the annuity are not taxed until money is withdrawn. Annuities are unique financial products that have become increasingly popular among retiring Americans who are drawn to guarantees, coupled with better returns than typical bank CDs.

Interestingly, while they may seem to be an invention of the modern banking world, annuities can be traced back to the days of ancient Rome when such contracts were known as *annua* (Latin for "annual stipends"). Roman citizens would make a one-time payment to the *annua*, in exchange for annual payments that would last their lifetime. These financial contracts were issued by the Emperor to raise capital.

In the 17th century, the countries of Europe, who seemed to always be fighting each other, came up with a variation on the Roman idea as a way to pay for their expensive wars. It was called the *tontine*, named after Lorenzo de Tontini, who is credited with inventing it in France in 1653. The way a tontine worked was kind of like a lottery with a twist. Participants paid in a lump sum, nonreturnable amount, in return for a guaranteed lifetime payout that began right away. The twist was that as the participants died off, the countries that issued the tontines paid the proceeds out to fewer and fewer people. The last few people alive did very well, and the last person standing did very well indeed. The last survivor of one French tontine lived to be 96. She put in 300 livres, which was the official currency of France until 1795, and was receiving an annual income of 73,000 livres when she died. In 2012 dollars, that's around $1.5 million.

Annuities Come To America

Annuities came to America during the colonial days when, in 1759, a Presbyterian synod formed the "Corporation for Relief of Poor and Distressed Widows and Children of Presbyterian Ministers." The ministers made regular contributions to the fund in exchange for what amounted to a pension. Other churches copied the idea. Soon, non-profit groups were making annuities available for the benefit of craftsmen and guild members. The first commercial offering of annuities came in 1912 when a Pennsylvania firm called "Company for Insurance on Lives and Granting Annuities" offered the idea to the public.

The sale of annuity contracts started to catch on in the 1930s, during the Great Depression, when insurance companies were seen as stable institutions after several bank failures. Because annuities were offered by insurance companies, they were afforded tax-deferred status, which enabled annuity owners to profit from the time value of money.

The first variable annuity came along in 1952. Variable annuities allowed interest to be credited based on the performance of separate accounts. These annuities contained risk because the money was subject to the ebb and flow of the stock market, but they were still insurance products and hence enjoyed the same tax-favored status, as did fixed annuities (same as today's annuities).

In those days, annuities had few bells and whistles. Today's annuities can be purchased with options that will provide nursing home benefits, a guaranteed lifetime income, checkbook access and return of premium, just to name a few. Surrender periods average 10 years or less. While no two annuities are the same, most provide penalty-free withdrawals for up to 10% of the account balance per year. Some offer loans of up to 50% of the value of the annuity, if a need arises. Today, annuity sales are estimated to be over $200 billion per year.

Variable Annuities

Some with whom I have spoken were not aware that *some* annuities come with risk and others do not. With variable annuities, for example, you get the returns of the stock market – both up and down. Don't get me wrong. Variable annuities have their place as investment vehicles for some, but they are not for everybody. They especially may not be suitable for an investor with a low risk tolerance. As the name suggests, variable annuities can vary in performance, and they can lose value.

It's always fun when the market is going up. But it is not so fun when the market is going down. A section of the "fine print" in a variable annuity contract may read, *"The Account Value is separate from the Protected Withdrawal Value, has no guarantee, may fluctuate, and can lose value."* That's an important little detail to understand, wouldn't you say? If you like the adventure of the stock market, then no worries. But if you don't like roller coaster thrill rides, then it may be time for an annuity rescue. If you are in or nearing retirement, you probably want something that is, as the title of this book suggests, *ridiculously reliable*…not risky and uncertain.

An annuity rescue here would probably involve a tax-free rollover from the variable annuity into something we call a *Retirement Income Annuity.* The RIA eliminates the ups and downs and the high tide/low tide market fluctuation and replaces it with a strategy that takes into consideration your new status as a retiree. (Special note* You don't have to be retired or near retirement to take advantage of an RIA. It is available to anyone over 40.) In this program you are insulated from market loss, but you are still able to share in the gains of the market up to a cap. When the market skyrockets, you will not get the total gains of that upswing. But when the market sinks like a stone, you don't lose. You advance and protect.

A relatively new feature is available on many of these programs. It is a special attachment that provides a guaranteed compound interest growth of between 5% and 7% for a lifetime retirement income.

Fixed Annuities

Some people may find themselves trapped in an underperforming fixed annuity that guarantees a fixed rate of interest for a set number of years. Again, these are fine instruments and useful for meeting certain financial objectives, but if you are saving money, chances are you are saving it for the future. Thus, if you have a specific income need in the future, your goal is probably to try to save enough to meet that need. Unfortunately, many of the fixed annuities that I see in portfolios today are lacking in the horsepower to meet the income needs of those who own them.

An annuity rescue here would mean looking for a more suitable program that would allow us to solve for income while still keeping the element of safety on our side. The Retirement Income Annuity with the guaranteed lifetime income attachment may be a good fit here as well. But no rescue is advisable if it comes with a penalty. No rollover would be acceptable if it created a taxable event or a penalty.

Planning adequately for the future often involves knowing where we stand at present with our finances. If we have money saved for retirement but it's not in a safe place or if it is not growing at an appropriate rate for our needs, then consider moving it as we approach that red zone of retirement.

Fixed Indexed Annuities

The Fixed *Indexed* Annuity (FIA) is a type of fixed annuity. It provides a minimum rate of interest, just like the traditional fixed annuity that we might call a "floor." But what makes it different, and what gives it greater earnings potential, is the fact that the performance of a specified stock index, usually the S&P 500, is used to calculate returns over that minimum. That is great! But hold the confetti for just a moment. There are caps ranging between 4% and 8%. If the S&P jumps up 20% in one year, your growth will hit that cap and stop. The caps are a tradeoff for having guarantee of principle. Thus, if the index loses 20%, the value of your FIA is not negatively affected.

FIA's are growing in popularity because they enable people to share in the upside of the Stock Market with absolutely no downside risk. Another attractive feature is the ratchet-reset provision. At the contract's anniversary date, the growth is locked in and now that is the new high-water mark of the annuity that represents the new amount that you cannot lose.

Common Misconceptions

Liquidity - Annuities are not entirely liquid. You trade a measure of liquidity for guaranteed safety and guaranteed return on investment. But the idea put forth by some critics of the product that annuities are "illiquid" is silly. Just like CDs at a bank, there are penalties for early withdrawal. Most professionals in the know regard annuity surrender charges and annuity surrender periods as reasonable. Those who point to surrender fees as if they were some kind of "gotcha" rigged by insurance companies to illegitimately take money from poor, unsuspecting customers, are usually investment advisors who do not offer such products. I think the term for such criticism is "sour grapes."

Surrender fees are necessary. If the annuitant does not keep his money invested with the insurance company for an adequate period of time for the insurance company to make a profit, then the insurance company might be forced to sell an investment earlier than it had planned. So, for the insurance company to guarantee the interest rate it promised, and guarantee safety of the principle, it has to set certain limits regarding withdrawals. The usual time limit, as mentioned earlier, is 10 years or less. They are called "10-year walk-aways" in the insurance industry, because after 10 years you have no surrender charges. You can walk away from the contract if you wish. Move your money, spend your money, reinvest your money or put it into another annuity. During the 10-year surrender period, is your money locked away and untouchable? No way. First of all, you have the 10% free (without penalty) withdrawals offered by most contracts. Secondly, the surrender charges are lower every year. They are highest during the first year of the contract, ranging anywhere from 6% to 16% and decreasing each year until they reach zero.

Guarantees – Sometimes detractors of annuities will say that they are not FDIC insured. That is true. They are an insurance product, not a bank product. They fall under an entirely different protection arrangement known as the Guaranty Association. Each state has a different one. These associations guarantee the funds invested with insurance companies in the rare event that an insurance company has financial difficulties. This arrangement is made possible by government regulations that require insurance companies to put money in reserves to cover any risk they undertake. The amount of protection varies by state, but in most cases the amount of protection, dollar for dollar, is more than that offered for bank accounts.

Fees and Commissions – Contrary to opinions proffered by those who do not offer fixed and fixed indexed annuities, no fees are charged within these products. Not so with the variable annuities customarily offered by brokers and bankers. Variable annuities do charge fees because they are usually invested in mutual funds, which contain fees called "loads." With variable annuities, you will still pay these fees, as well as the broker or banker's commissions, even if your variable annuity loses money.

On the other hand, fixed and fixed indexed annuities have no risk, no fees and no commissions that come out of your balance. Any commissions paid to agents are paid by the insurance carriers that produce the product.

As to how fixed and fixed indexed annuity agents are paid, think of a travel agent. If you book your trip through a competent travel agent, you will likely be dealing with someone who possesses a vast knowledge of the industry and who can plan for you a worry-free vacation at a lower cost than you could have found had you planned the trip yourself. The airline companies and the hotels pay the travel agent, not you.

Know Your Options

If I could build this next sentence out of 30-foot tall cinderblock letters and paint it Day-Glo orange, I would – *Annuities are not for everyone!* And I strongly urge you to never put all of your assets into an annuity, regardless of how great it appears to be. You should always approach making a decision to purchase an annuity by first having a thorough, holistic review of your finances. You should then consider all your options. Seek the help of a fiduciary, not a salesperson.

Annuities can be fine instruments for income planning and great for retirement planning, but only if they are suitable for your individual circumstances and they match your individual financial goals.

CHAPTER TEN

What Is Holistic Financial Planning?

"Never go to a doctor whose office plants have died."
— Erma Bombeck

One sign I have never seen in the window of a shoe store is, *"One Size Fits All."* The reason is simple. Feet come in all different sizes. When it comes to income planning for retirement, however, some professionals treat all cases with the same formulaic approach. It is insensitive and inefficient at best, and hazardous to one's wealth at worst, which is why I recommend Holistic Financial Planning instead.

Holistic derives from the Greek word, *holos,* which means "whole." As the sound of the word suggests, holism is treating or attending to the "whole" of a thing, as opposed to its isolated parts. A holistic approach to anything recognizes that all its parts are connected and interrelated. As a philosophy, holism is becoming a popular approach in education, medicine and the sciences. In medicine, for example, the concept calls for examining all aspects of the patient's needs, psychological, physical and social, and taking them all into account before any treatment is undertaken. Practically, it is recognizing that stress can cause hypertension. A pill may lower blood pressure, but it is a temporary fix. To get at the real problem, find what's causing the stress and try to eliminate that.

Holistic financial planning recognizes that money is only green wrinkled paper and numbers on a page until it is translated into what you want the money to do for you and those you love. Holistic financial planning recognizes that you can't get the most out of your money without first knowing what purpose the money is to serve. A holistic financial planner will spend time, especially during the first interview with a client, listening to the client's desires, dreams, goals, objectives and passions so the planner's recommendations are on target with those things. A holistic financial planner will often use a team of professionals, ranging from certified public accountants to estate attorneys, to get the job done.

Every case is different because every client is different. It may be the passion of one client to leave a legacy for his children and grandchildren, whereas another client wants to spend as much as possible, living the good life in his sunset years. The holistic financial planner will know that before recommending any course of action that involves the client's assets. Holistic financial planning is becoming more and more popular – not because it is easy for the planner. The fact is, holistic financial planning requires more effort and thought on the part of the planner. Holistic planning is becoming more popular because the baby boom generation, which is more insistent on good service from its professionals in many other fields, seems to insist on it.

Knowing What You Want

A good doctor will examine a patient more with questions than a he or she will a stethoscope. A good doctor will listen and analyze the answers in the light of information gathered about the patient. Then, finally, once the information has painted a clear and complete picture of the patient's health, a treatment or a remedy can be recommended – a well thought out strategy aimed at overall healing and well-being, not just a feel-good pill.

For any of that to happen, however, the patient needs to first answer the doctor's questions.

When it comes to financial planning, the client must help the financial advisor understand the condition of his wealth by supplying the appropriate financial documents that will acquaint the advisor with the client's current financial position. In short, after knowing the client's goals and aspirations regarding his wealth, the holistic financial planner needs to know specifically how much money the client has and how it is positioned before the advisor can help. Clarifying today's asset picture helps establish our starting place.

There are choices to be made, too. What do I want my money to do for me? In detail, what lifestyle do I plan to have once I retire? Am I interested in leaving a legacy to my loved ones? If so, who are they, and what form will it take?

One of my favorite Yogi Berra quotations goes like this – "You've got to be very careful if you don't know where you're going, because you might not get there." Financial goals have to be meaningful specifics and not wandering generalities. It is imperative to nail down what your income needs will be for the rest of your life in retirement, making sure to account for inflation and contingencies. Be as specific as you possibly can. A holistic financial planner will be able to work backwards from that number and remove the guesswork from the equation. He or she will begin with fact-finding and end with solutions that fit your unique situation – not try to find a convenient cookie-cutter formula that requires the least effort on the advisor's part.

Holistic Planning is Tailored To You

Morey Amsterdam, famous co-star of the Dick Van Dyke Show, popular in the 1960s, was famous for his dry wit. He told the joke about a man who goes into a rip-off clothing store to buy a suit. He tries the suit on, but it's a terrible fit. The coat is too big, and the pants are way too long. The crafty salesman, eager to move the merchandise, tells him to hike up the trousers with his right hand. He does.

"But the coat is too big," says the man.

"Take your left hand and pull it tighter," says the salesman.

"Now the collar doesn't fit," complains the shopper.

"Hold it down with your chin," says the salesman. "Now it fits perfectly!"

The man walks out of the store, wearing the ill-fitting suit he has just purchased, his body contorted to hold it in place. Two doctors pass him by on the sidewalk. "What do you think is wrong with that poor guy?" the first one asks. "I don't know," says the other, "but doesn't his suit fit nicely?"

The point is that if the financial plan we have does not fit our needs for the present and our goals for the future, let's face the facts and get a second opinion. For example, let's say the proposed financial plan reads like this – "At this *projected* rate of growth you can *probably* expect a *projected* income of *approximately* $60,000 per year for *approximately* 20 years." Sorry, but that suit just doesn't fit. There are too many uncertainties. Programs do exist in today's financial marketplace that take the "probably" and "projected" off the page and replace it with words like "guaranteed" and "unlimited." A holistic financial planner will know where to find those financial instruments and determine if they are a good fit for you and your unique circumstances

Plan With Longevity in View

No one knows how many heartbeats he or she is given in this life. There is no computer program that can predict how much sand is in one's hourglass. Statistically, we are living longer, and we should plan with that in mind. At this writing, the average American's lifespan is 84. More and more Americans are making it into their 90s and beyond. Any financial plan that has you running out of money prematurely is forcing upon you the idea of forfeiting your independence, and becoming either a ward of the state or a burden upon your family. For most, those alternatives are just not acceptable.

Like the man buying the suit, some do not know that they have many choices available to them when it comes to income planning for retirement. Getting a second opinion from a retirement income specialist usually costs nothing but a little time. It may be time well spent, however, if in the process, you discover a retirement plan that has built in safe money returns that cannot expire.

Summary
Baby Step Four: Making Your Own Way

It would be marvelous if there were some government program to take care of us forever. The truth is, however, there just is not. For the vast millions of Americans, "If it is to be, it is up to me." If we want a dependable, steady and inexhaustible income stream during retirement, we are on our own, and we must start planning now. Think in terms of turning your savings and investments into a perpetually moving water wheel of money that will steadily produce an income we cannot outlive.

When it comes to a lifetime income stream, think of buckets of money, each put to work at differing rates of return. While one pays out its income, others are gaining interest for future years. A competent retirement income specialist can explain how such a system works. It may surprise you how far your savings will take you if properly positioned.

There are all kinds of annuities out there. If you happen to be trapped in an underperforming fixed annuity, or you are perhaps in over your head with a risky variable annuity, then get a second opinion. You may be due for an annuity rescue. Look for one that has one of the relatively new lifetime income provisions that are sweeping the country for those approaching or in retirement.

You do not go to an auto mechanic for a heart problem. Nor do you see a doctor for a car problem. Make sure your plan for retirement is tailor-made and custom fitted for you and your unique circumstances. Holistic financial planners will look at the overall picture before making any recommendations. Because we are all different individuals, with different dreams, different goals and separate financial objectives, there is no "one-size-fits-all" approach when it comes to finding a ridiculously reliable retirement income plan.

Step Five

Looking Ahead

CHAPTER ELEVEN

Planning for the Unexpected

"To expect the unexpected shows a thoroughly modern intellect."
– Oscar Wilde

I have what my wife, Kim, calls an unreasonable disdain for toll roads. It used to be that when I traveled in the northeastern United States, I would carry about $30 worth of change with me. The quarters, dimes, and nickels sat in a soft leather pouch on the console between the passenger seat and the driver's seat. When we rolled into the toll area, I either had my change ready to fling at the basket, or bills in hand to pay the person in the toll booth. Nowadays, I try to avoid the rat's nest of pay highways in that part of the country by setting my GPS to find alternate routes. I have always viewed toll booths as a money-grubbing nuisance which, if I had my way, I would declare all roads free and eliminate the entire lot of them.

I have given some thought about this little hang up of mine, and I have come to the conclusion that there are two reasons why I have it. One has to do with the principles of thrift instilled in me by my parents. Paying to drive is like paying to breathe. Another reason has to do with an experience my father and I had with a toll basket in New Jersey when I was around nine years old.

Our drive that day took us through one toll booth after another. In time, the manned stations gave way to the newer automated stations – the ones with baskets that would catch the coins you threw into it. Whenever my father saw the sign that read, "Pay Toll Ahead", he began digging through his pockets for change. At one particular toll booth, however, he searched every pocket without results. The toll roads had (pardon the pun) taken their toll. Dad was completely out of money.

"Do you have any change in your pocket, Peter?" he asked hopefully.

I shook my head, wishing I could help.

The lanes widened as we approached the toll baskets. Dad selected an empty chute and pulled in. We were supposed to stop on red, give the machine its due, and then take off when the light turned green. My father stopped the car, shrugged his shoulders and just drove through the red light. What else was there to do? He couldn't throw anything at the basket, because there just wasn't anything to throw.

The New Jersey State Trooper pulled us over about a mile down the highway. "It must have missed the basket," my father said, as the officer nonchalantly continued writing out the ticket.

Avoiding Life's Toll Booths

On life's highway, there can be many unpleasant interruptions and roadblocks that can impede our journey and serve as sources of irritation. We can avoid many of them by planning ahead. Personal Global Positioning Systems were something out of Buck Rogers when my father and I had our little run-in with the New Jersey State Police. Today, a small 4" by 5" box could have steered us around that situation. Other such encounters can be dealt with by simply preparing for them, just as our troubles could have been avoided by taking along enough money for the tolls.

Divorce

There are some life events we don't prepare for because we can't envision them ever happening to us. No couple thinks of divorce during the ceremony, or when the music is playing afterward. It's the furthest thing from the minds of the happy couple. But almost half of all American couples who marry, end up getting divorced. So it is a fact of life.

In April 2012, the National Center for Family & Marriage Research released a study on the "Gray Divorce Revolution" that said divorce rates are higher for members of the baby boom generation than for any previous generation and that an unprecedented number of Americans are splitting up after turning 50. The study revealed that one in four divorces involve adults over 50, whereas in 1990, the statistics were one in 10. That's quite a jump.

Longevity plays a factor. With 60 being the new 40, an age where many boomers feel like life is just beginning for them, a relationship that has lasted under stress for 20 or 30 years might just not have the staying power it once did when you were "over the hill" at 50.

The financial fallout from divorce in later years is considerable. Let's face it, the longer the couple has been together, the more assets they possess and the more complicated things become when there has to be a division of those assets with retirement right around the corner.

The reason why I bring this up here is not to pass judgment or cause trouble. I mention it simply to point out one potential "toll booth" that might impede you on your road to retirement and to help you know how to deal with it. Divorce may feel like the right thing to do emotionally, but I would be remiss as a financial counselor if I didn't encourage anyone contemplating divorce to count the cost. In these uncertain economic times, happy endings are not always the end of the story. Consider these things:

- In unsettled economic times, older single people face more economic hardships than do married couples.
- If the divorce happens during a time when property values are down (buyer's market), a forced sale of jointly owned property may cost each participant in the divorce thousands of dollars.
- Retirement accounts, 401(k)s, 403(b)s, TSP's and any other retirement account gets split between the couple.

There are some exceptions, but in many cases, the division of assets in a divorce will be fifty-fifty. It is an emotional time, and people who make critical money decisions in a highly charged emotional atmosphere, may regret them later. When one party to the divorce is awarded half the assets in the other party's qualified retirement program, for example, he or she may not consider that they have just been awarded a tax time bomb. I have seen cases where one spouse may view this as a nice little consolation prize for having put up with "that jerk" for 20 years, and blow the proceeds on a shopping spree. Spending the money may make them feel good temporarily, but at the end of the year, when they get a nice little letter from Uncle Sam reminding them that they now owe taxes on the entire amount, the good feeling is gone. Had they seen a financial professional beforehand, they would have most likely learned that any money received from a qualified account, such as a 401(k) or 403(b), should be rolled over into another qualified account or transferred into a self-directed IRA.

Another mistake happens when, in order to pay the tax bill, the divorced mate digs the hole deeper by dipping into his or her retirement savings again to pay the unexpected tax bill. That is called a "double whammy," because there will be yet another tax bill for the additional funds used to pay taxes.

People can often go wrong when they play catch-up. Let's say that you were the responsible mate – the one who did everything you were supposed to do. You made sure to contribute the maximum from your paycheck into your retirement plan. Your spouse, on the other hand, saved nary a penny and selfishly blew whatever money he or she had. Now divorce happens. Your $400,000 401(k) is now worth $200,000. You now have half the money you thought would be available for retirement. Unfortunately, some will, at this point, try to play catch-up and put more of their assets at risk than they should. See a retirement income specialist. Remember the rule of 100. Put a percent sign after your age and this is the percentage of your assets you should keep absolutely safe. In fact, because of your unique circumstances, add 10% to it. In other words, if you are age 50, then have 60% of your assets protected from market loss. Talk to someone who specializes in retirement income planning. There are still places out there where your money will grow and still be insulated from the volatility of the fickle stock market.

If you were accustomed to letting your spouse make all the money decisions, then you probably need a financial plan that doesn't require you to always have your hand on the wheel. You will probably be best served by a financial plan that can be placed on automatic pilot.

"He Handles The Money"

In many marriages it is not uncommon for one spouse to handle all the financial affairs, while the other spouse has little knowledge of such things as investment accounts, retirement strategies, budgets and the like. It is not that the one spouse necessarily wishes to keep the other one in the dark – in some relationships, things just happen that way. I know of many marriages where the kitchen is the domain of one and not the other. Sometimes one mate has a passion for the garden and the lawn, and the other mate isn't at all interested in such things. Caring for the money in the family becomes a household duty of one and not the other by default in some cases.

"He makes the money, and I spend it," laughed one woman. Referring to the couple's finances, she said, "I don't even need to know where the checkbook is; I use credit cards."

She wasn't kidding, either. She really didn't know where the checkbook was. If something were to have happened to her husband, she would have been hard pressed to find the documents necessary to carry on an independent life. I know of other cases where the roles are just the opposite. It's the wife who pays attention to all things financial and the husband is the one who is in the dark.

In households where this is the case, I recommend that the spouse who handles the finances keep a simple notebook and leave it in a place where the other spouse can easily locate it at any time. The notebook can contain a list of financial institutions where money is deposited or invested, and the phone numbers of those institutions. The notebook might also contain passwords to computer programs that are used to manage those accounts or view balances. If sensitive information such as passwords is kept in the notebook, it is advisable to keep the notebook in a safe. You can usually buy a small, fireproof safe for around $100. Oh, yes! I almost forgot. Make the combination to the safe something that he or she absolutely cannot forget, like the date of your marriage, or a variation on that theme. That way, it is not only romantic, but practical.

When That Spouse Dies

In light of the foregoing, it is easy to see why the death of a spouse who handles the money in the family can be financially traumatic. Emotions are involved. The person quarterbacking your retirement plan is gone. Perhaps your relationship with the financial planner either just wasn't there or it wasn't one that you cared for. Either way, you feel on your own. Hopefully, trusted family members can be of help at a time like this. But it seems that nothing stirs up trouble among family members more than jealousy over money. No matter what, this can be a difficult time.

This can be a time when sharks appear. It is a time to exercise caution if you are a bereaved spouse who now has to cope with financial matters with which you are unfamiliar. Sure, it's a time when you need friends, but when "friends" begin taking an undue interest in your financial affairs, it should signal caution. It could be argued that someone who pries too deeply into personal matters during the grieving process is hurting more than helping.

Aside from handling the necessary arrangements that go with losing a loved one, such as funeral arrangements and locating important documents, you may wish to take a "time out" for a month or so. Take a few steps back until you are past the initial phase of the grieving process. If money decisions are awaiting your attention, wait until the time is right and get two or three opinions from those inside your circle of trust before making significant money decisions.

Seek the Help of a Fiduciary

When seeking the help of a professional, make sure that he or she is a fiduciary. Being a fiduciary means the person is bound by both law and ethics to act for another person's benefit and not his own. Fiduciary responsibility is a very serious obligation in the eyes of the justice system. Fiduciaries must act on your behalf, putting your needs and interests ahead of their own. If they don't, they could face legal trouble for their actions.

One of the most important questions you could ask of a financial planner is, "Are you a fiduciary?" Ask if the individual is licensed with the state as a fiduciary. Don't accept a verbal answer; ask for proof in writing that this is the case. No one wants to appear distrustful, but asking this question of a bona fide financial professional will not be taken as an insult. Asking to see credentials is perfectly acceptable when large sums of money are involved.

Some financial professionals may be perfectly legitimate in their field of expertise, but may specialize only in selling and buying shares of stock. They may not be acquainted with income strategies, wills, trusts and tax planning. If that is the case, then knowing that right away will prevent misunderstandings.

Trust, But Verify

When a spouse dies and money decisions need to be made, trust is a huge factor. Those who are acquainted with the customs of the South know that in antebellum days, to question someone's truthfulness was tantamount to questioning one's honor and was an automatic invitation to a duel. Regardless of where you live, it is only human nature to want to display a trusting spirit. But sometimes, nothing draws out the worst in people like the smell of money. It is prudent to establish verifiable trust before making any serious decisions about money after a spouse dies.

I am fond of something Ronald Reagan said when dealing with the Soviets on arms negotiation back in the 1980s. He was a master at using few words to make a point. Knowing that it was part of the Russian culture to speak with many proverbs, he borrowed a saying from Soviet revolutionary Vladimir Lenin and used it frequently, speaking in Russian, when discussing the language of a treaty being hammered out by the two nations. The proverb was, ""doveryai, no proveryai," the English translation of which is "Trust, but verify."
The expression was picked up by the media and became a signature phrase of the negotiations. It is a wise proverb and a prudent course to take whenever money is involved, especially at times when emotions run high. American/Irish humorist Peter Finley Dunne perhaps said it best, "Trust everybody, but cut the cards."

CHAPTER TWELVE

Planning for and Caring for Your Parents

"Caring for our seniors is perhaps the greatest responsibility we have. Those who walked before us have given so much and made possible the life we all enjoy." – John Hoeven

W hen it comes to care giving, the baby boom generation is unique. Perhaps because boomers are living longer and perhaps because of social changes in the last century, many of those now nearing retirement find themselves caring for their children and their parents at the same time. Needless to say, this can be a financial burden. But there are certain things that you should do, and other things that you should not do in this regard. One thing to avoid, if at all possible, is dipping into your personal retirement savings to help either a child or a parent. It is not advisable for several reasons.

In retirement accounts that are tax deferred, you will owe taxes on any money you withdraw. In most cases, if you withdraw money before reaching age 59 ½, you will also pay a 10% penalty on the amount withdrawn. If those two reasons aren't good enough to leave those accounts alone, consider this: Your retirement savings is probably growing at compound interest. If you take money out, even if you fully intend to replace it down the road, you have lost not only the money taken out, but also the *time value* of that money. You have literally lost those years of compound interest. Why is that so important? Because compound interest means that not only does your money grow, but also the interest gains interest as well. In many cases, it would be better to borrow money instead of dipping into your retirement fund. Any years that go by without those dollars working for you are lost forever.

To illustrate how just losing a small section of time from a time-sensitive account can make a large difference, consider what would happen if an airplane flying from Los Angeles to New York City were one degree off course. For every sixty miles the plane flies forward, it flies one mile off target.

I use this illustration sometimes at events where I am asked to give talks on preparing for retirement. When I posed the question to one group, a quick thinker near the front said, "Your plane would get shot down."

Curious, I asked him to explain.

"Well, if you kept flying off course like that and didn't correct it, the Air Force would scramble some jets and take you out, thinking you were a terrorist or something."

I got it.

It makes the point anyway, doesn't it? If you don't want your retirement "shot down," stay on course with it. It is amazing what a difference one degree will make.

Helping Older Parents Make Decisions

Your parents may be in a situation where they are up in years and perhaps vulnerable when it comes to decisions pertaining to money and health care. Let's face it, older people fall for the "slick-talking" salesperson more readily than younger folks. It could be they don't hear quite as well as they once did and don't want to acknowledge it when they fail to understand something. Also, older adults are sometimes more easily intimidated when a salesperson befriends them and then uses high pressure tactics to close the sale.

It is simply a good idea to encourage your parents to adopt a 48-hour rule when it comes to making any decisions that require a signature. Take two full days to relax and think about it. They will be able to use that time to consult with someone within their circle of trust – someone who has their best interests at heart – before making a significant decision on anything.

Decisions regarding long-term care can be difficult for your parents if they are advanced in years and are not capable of making such decisions on their own. It is advisable to have those kinds of discussions long before the long-term care is needed. When money is involved, the subject may often be more easily broached with the help of a third party professional, such as an elder law attorney. He or she will be able to help you prepare whatever legal paperwork that will be necessary to make a fluid transition to a care facility when the time comes. The attorney will be able help you put in place such documents as a health care power of attorney, living will and anything else that is needed.

Nursing home care, as of this writing, averages between $70,000 and $80,000 per year, and over 50% of those who enter a facility, will stay longer than a year. Misconceptions abound as to who pays for this. Some think regular health insurance or Medicare will pay for it. But that's not so. On average, Medicare covers only about 2%, and private health insurance covers only 1% of nursing home costs. The latest research reveals that almost 70% of people 65 or older will need long-term care services at some point in their lives.

"Nobody wants to plan ahead for this," says Virginia Morris, a journalist who has written widely on the subject of aging. "But you will be so grateful you did it, because if you don't do it, you'll end up responding to one crisis after the next, and you are exhausted, and your parents will get mediocre care."

Experts contend that the time to bring up the subject of health care with parents is before it becomes "crisis driven." It is much easier to deal with a future situation than a current situation – when it can be regarded as planning for possible eventualities instead of handling an emergency.

Procrastination in this area helps no one. Your parents may not require help from you now, but sooner or later, they will likely be faced with receiving some kind of assistance. According to statistics from the U.S. Department of Health and Human Services, in 2000, there were 10 million people who needed help with activities of daily living, such as eating, bathing and dressing. By 2050 that number will more than double to 27 million.

What about Long-Term Care Insurance?

One of the enduring ironies about long-term care insurance is that when we can afford it, we don't think we need it. We are bulletproof and indestructible! By the time we come to be in touch with our own mortality, and realize the need for it, we can't afford it.

The insurance companies haven't made it any easier. For years, it has been a "use it or lose it" proposition. If you pay into a policy for decades, and then drop it, all those premium dollars are down the drain. What happens if you never need the care? With stand-alone, traditional long-term health care policies, there is no provision for having any of that money returned to you. If you live to a ripe old age and "die with your boots on," as the saying goes, the money you paid in premiums all those years certainly doesn't go to your heirs.

Another problem with long-term care policies sold decades ago was that they were mispriced. The premiums were too cheap. When carriers experience higher claims than they expected, in some cases where the contracts allowed, they raised premiums. This has forced some to drop polices they have had for years, because the premiums were no longer unaffordable.

But times are changing in this regard. There are many newer policies on the market these days that, while they aren't the traditional long-term care policies, address the same needs without becoming prohibitively expensive. Plainly stated, these new policies were developed because the old style "use-it-or-lose-it" offerings just weren't flying off the shelves. So to answer the complaints made by the burgeoning baby boom generation, a new breed of life insurance and annuity contracts began arriving on the market around the year 2000. These policies provide long-term care benefits *when and if you need them*, but allow you to keep the money you put into the annuity or life insurance policy if you don't.

One annuity, for example, will give you a lifetime income that doubles if you need long-term care in a nursing home. It is not a true long-term care policy, and it may not cover all the expenses associated with long-term care, but it's better than having nothing at all.

Some new life insurance policies will let you dip into the death benefit while you are still alive, if you need the money to cover long-term care expenses. If you don't use it for long-term care, then the death benefit stays intact. This seems to make a lot of sense. If you need the care, why not go ahead and use some of the death benefit and put yourself in charge of how and where that care is administered. Otherwise, if you left those decisions up to your family members, they would likely foot the bill and then, upon your death, receive the death benefit to reimburse them. This way, however, you can be more in charge of your own affairs.

One good thing about America is that the free enterprise system hates a vacuum. If there is a need out there, it will soon be filled. Some enterprising soul will come along and make sure that every itch has a scratcher. That phenomenon holds true in the world of insurance, too. When companies began to realize that the traditional "use it or lose it" approach to long-term care insurance wasn't attracting customers, they put on their thinking caps and invited their actuaries to the table to design contracts that would be more of a win/win situation for both the company and the policy holder. One result was a hybrid life insurance policy that has been steadily growing in popularity in the insurance marketplace. In some respects, it resembles a CD at the bank. You put in a lump sum, and if you need long-term care in the future, it will give you back three to five times what you put in – just for that one life event, long-term care expense. If you put in $100,000, for example, and you need long-term care in the future, you could get $400,000 or so back in increments as specified in the policy. If you die without needing long-term care, then the benefit turns into life insurance. Approximately one and a half times what you put into the policy is paid out as a tax-free death benefit to your heirs. The terms of the coverage will vary depending on your age, your health, and whether you are male or female, which is why you may find it advisable to meet with a qualified, trusted advisor to see if such a plan would be suitable for you and your unique circumstances.

Some new style annuities allow you to put in a lump sum, say $100,000, which will grow at around 3% or 4% interest, but, in the meantime, should you need long-term health care, you would be able to receive up to three times that amount in benefits. These plans have become quite popular with the latest crop of retirees who, having thumbed their noses at stand-alone long-term care policies because they were so expensive, are now in the market for some kind coverage. These are the same retirees who don't want to fork over the high-dollar premiums that the coverage would cost at their age. There are some tradeoffs. These new annuities are not going to get you rich quick by any means. The interest rates are better than bank CDs, but they are still pretty conservative. If you don't need long-term care, they behave as would any other fixed annuity. In the parlance of the insurance world, they are often called "combos," and your financial advisor should be aware of them. They should also be able to explain the details to you and determine if they are suitable.

CHAPTER THIRTEEN

Planning for and Caring for Your Children

*"The easiest way to teach children the value of money
is to borrow some from them."*
- Anonymous

W e had the "beatniks" of the 1950s, the "hippies" of the 1960s and the "yuppies" of the 1970s. Now we are seeing something called the "sandwich" generation emerge. This group finds itself in the awkward position of preparing kids to leave the nest, taking care of elderly parents, and trying to plan for their own retirement.

Studies conducted by the Pew Research Center confirm that as of 2012, roughly one out of every eight Americans aged 40-60 is still caring for both their children and at least one parent. United States Census Bureau statistics indicate that the number of older Americans (over 65) will double to more than 70 million by the year 2030. It is not uncommon for baby boomers to be caring for one child at home, putting another through college and looking for a nursing home for one or both of their parents.

Paying for College

Providing our children with a college education is part of the American dream, but American parents are getting a bad case of sticker shock when confronted with the cost of higher education. The cost of attending a four-year *private* university now averages more than $37,000 per year. That includes tuition, fees and lodging. Four-year *public* universities cost more than $18,000 per year, on average. The average cost of attending a two-year public college has now reached $14,000 per year. The killer is that costs are increasing by about 8% per year. The fact remains, however, that getting a college education is essential for most to pursue the American dream of getting a good job, owning a home and raising a family. So, even though the cost of a college education is high, the cost of foregoing it is even higher.

In order to help pay for their education, students are taking on debt loads that would have been unthinkable when their parents went to school. Nationally, the student loan debt topped $1 trillion in 2011, eclipsing credit card debt for the first time.

Just as there are retirement planning strategies that can save you thousands of dollars, there are strategies that can save you thousands when it comes to paying for college.

Financial Aid

Many think that financial aid is only for needy families. Not true. As a financial advisor, it pains me greatly to see how much money slips through the hands of students and their parents because they don't know how the system works. By not helping their children take advantage of grants, scholarships and financial aid, some parents unknowingly forfeit their security in retirement. More than $125 billion in financial aid is distributed each year and, if you are sending kids to college, some of it may have your family's name on it. In theory, the federal financial aid system is based on need, but in practice and in reality, you don't have to be needy to get it…you just have to know how the system works. Don't think its welfare. It's your tax dollars at work. Your congressmen and senators have put the rules in place by which you can obtain it.

Federal financial aid comes in many varieties. Nearly 70% of student financial aid is provided by the U.S. Department of Education's Federal Student Aid (FSA) program and consists of grants, loans or work-study programs.

Grants don't have to be paid back and they are a great way to help pay for college. Grants can come from private organizations, such as churches and civic groups. They may be awarded by professional organizations, seeking to advance their cause in the world. They may even come from the educational institution itself. Yes, the school charges you on the one hand but offers you a way to pay on the other. And, of course, state and federal governments offer grants. These grants may be awarded based on a student's race, religion, special interests, or his or her financial need.

Sadly, billions of dollars that are available in grants from both private and government sources go un-awarded because people don't know how to apply for them. We live in a paperwork world, and just saying the word "application" makes us flinch. But many of these applications can be filled out online. If you are somewhat computer savvy, just throw a few key words at your favorite search engine, and you will come up with thousands of sites containing information on how to apply for these grants.

Scholarships

Those good grades your kids are getting in high school could be worth thousands of dollars when applying for college. Educational institutions look at grades and standardized test scores in their admissions process, but that's not all those scores and grades are used for. They are also considered when colleges and universities make financial aid decisions as well. Just 10 points higher on an SAT score could be worth thousands of dollars. Why? Universities are businesses. They want students with high test scores, and they are willing to compete to get them. How? By offering students better financial aid packages. Money spent getting tutored for the SAT or similar standardized tests, is money invested.

When families are deciding what university their children will attend, they often make the incorrect assumption that the pricey private schools are beyond their reach. It may surprise you to know that many of these schools have increased their aid budgets, and some so-called elite schools are less expensive than public universities. There are web sites now that will give you a complete rundown by school of both cost and offsetting financial aid. It pays to shop around.

Getting your family's fair share of the billions of dollars in merit aid on the table comes down to the scholastic performance of your children. Colleges compete for "A" students by giving what amounts to discounts off their "sticker" price. It is not unusual to open a school's website and find what amounts to an advertisement posted, offering small scholarships for academic performance. One school, in order to attract high performers from other universities, offered what they called a "Transfer President's Scholarship" – $7,000 for students who "distinguished themselves" in either college or high school. This school left open for discussion what it meant to have "distinguished" oneself. That means they will review the applications and take the ones they want.

Other colleges will spell out the criteria, such as "$4,000 Provost Award" for students who graduated in the top 10% of their class or have a Grade Point Average of 3.75 or better.

The point is…scholarships are out there. You have to look for them, and compete for them. There is no limit to how many small scholarships you can obtain. Every free dollar helps when it comes to paying for education. Some crazy scholarships we have seen:

- **Civil War Veteran Scholarship** – $1,000 if you are a descendant of a veteran of the Civil War. You have to write an essay.
- **Extreme Sports Scholarships** – One school offered $8,000 based on your skateboarding skills.
- **Tall Person Scholarship** – $1,000 if you are male and over 6'2", or female and 5'10" or taller. You have to write an essay on "What Being Tall Means to Me."
- **Potato Scholarship** – The National Potato Council awards annually one $5,000 scholarship to a graduate student pursuing Agribusiness, which enhances the potato industry.
- **The American Fire Sprinkler Association Scholarship** – Compete for $2,000 by reading an essay about fire sprinklers and taking a 10-question test.
- **Bowling Scholarship** – The United States Bowling Association offers a number of scholarships to bowling fans with dollar amounts ranging from $1,000 to $2,500.
- **Star Trek Scholarship** – If you are an active member of the Starfleet Academy (a club of Star Trek fans) and attend any type of post-high school learning institution, you could receive a $500 scholarship.
- **Zolp Scholarship** – If you were born with the last name Zolp and you happen to be Catholic, Loyola University will award you its Zolp Scholarship. The amount was unspecified, but any amount would be some compensation for being born with the last name Zolp.

Other Ways to Trim Costs

There are other inventive ways to trim the cost of obtaining a college education:

- **Cooperative education (co-op) programs** are offered by many universities that allow students to combine a job with their college education. It is way less expensive and often makes it easier to get hired after earning a degree.
- **Make appropriate adjustments in family assets.** Financial aid formulas favor some tax-deferred accounts. See a financial professional who is knowledgeable in this field to determine if moving some of your assets into a tax advantaged status may help qualify your student for financial aid.
- **Earn college credits while still in high school.** Take advanced placement (AP) classes if possible. Take "dual enrollment" classes if they are offered. You can take those credits with you when you start college. Look into CLEP (Col-

lege Level Examination Program) exams. Depending on the college and depending on your score, you may be able to trim a year out of the process.

• **Start with a Community College.** If you go for a couple of years to a community college and then transfer to a more expensive school, you will get the same diploma as everyone else and may have saved a considerable amount of money.

All things considered, money is only green, wrinkled paper and numbers on a page, unless it has a purpose. This is a book about retirement, not college planning or elder care. The reason for bringing it up here is because I see too many people forfeit a sound retirement plan because their resources are drained in an effort to keep up with obligations, either real or perceived, to other family members. How sad it is to see someone generous of spirit left in undesirable straits through lack of planning.

Those of the baby boom generation have witnessed many soul-stirring events thus far in their time on earth. From placing a man on the moon to the development of the Internet, these marvelous achievements have created a pervasive "anything's possible" mindset in this generation – something that their parents, whose lives were tempered by hard times of a world war and the Great Depression, lacked. The boom generation that has earned more money than any other generation in history, has also created more debt than any other generation in history. From where I watch the world, I sometimes see many of the "sandwich" generation bite off more than they can chew. As a professional planner, I work with budgets. From my experience in dealing with hundreds of situations, such as the ones described in the last two chapters of this book, I believe that by the simple act of categorizing and prioritizing, we can balance our load when it comes to caring for family members. In most cases, we can do right by them without killing our own chances of a reliable retirement plan in the process.

Summary
Baby Step Five: Looking Out Ahead

Life is full of unexpected events. They are like toll booths that can either be avoided or prepared for. It helps to take each area of our life and look out ahead – project to where our path could possibly take us, and be ready for the journey.

If we have family members, then those loved ones come with obligation tags that will be accounted for in different measure. It is as possible to inherit debt, as it is to inherit wealth. Much of what we inherit is beyond our control. How we handle the cards we are dealt in this respect, however, is something we can control.

Divorce and the death of a spouse can present its own brand of complications. Decisions made at a time when emotions are running high could cost us if we decide incorrectly. Take some time. Seek professional help.

Members of the "sandwich generation" are those baby boomers who find themselves raising children on the one hand, and caring for aging parents on the other. The more responsibility we have in this regard, the more carefully we should plan. Individuals in this situation may need a helping hand from other family members, or trusted professionals to ensure that they don't crack under the pressure and make decisions that cause them to forfeit their own sound financial future in the process of caring for others.

Avoid toll booths if possible. But if you can't avoid them, at least be prepared for them.

Step Six

Getting the Right Kind of Help

CHAPTER FOURTEEN

Finding the Right Financial Advice

"Wall Street is the only place that people ride to in a Rolls Royce to get advice from those who take the subway." – Warren Buffett

B orn in 1890, Victor Lustig, also known as "the man who sold the Eiffel Tower," was the most talented con man who ever lived. In terms of diabolical cleverness, he makes Bernie Madoff look like a kid stealing lunch money.

Lustig, a Czechoslovakian, would book passage on ocean liners sailing between Paris and New York City and run his "money printing machine" scam. Fluent in both English and French, he would allow others to observe him working the machine, but complaining about it. It seems that the darn thing printed perfect $100 bills, but it took way too long – around six hours – to print one bill. Sensing huge profits, some rich fool would buy the machine from him, usually for amounts of $30,000 or more. The machine would print $100 bills for the next day or so, until the cruise ended. Then, with Lustig long gone, it would produce only blank paper. The $100 bills Lustig's machine had dispensed earlier were real $100 bills, and the machine had been set to run out of them once Lustig disappeared.

Lustig's biggest con, the one involving the Eiffel Tower, took place in 1925. It was in the newspapers that year that Paris was having problems maintaining all the steel on the Eiffel Tower. Lustig took this opportunity to begin impersonating an official of the Paris government seeking bids from scrap metal dealers. Alas, the grand tower would have to be dismantled and sold to the highest bidder. He had his marks come, one at a time, to bid on the tower and, of course, produce a large cash deposit. By the time the defrauded businessmen figured out what had happened, the slick-talking Lustig was nowhere to be found, and the joke was on them.

While Lustig takes the top spot for cunning and cleverness, Madoff tops them all when it comes to volume. His Ponzi scheme was responsible for bilking $50 billion from trusting clients who had enjoyed their sweet returns too much to ask questions…until it was too late. Fortunately for us, the types of fraud that Madoff pulled off, as infamous as they may be, are actually quite rare. The vast majority of agencies, firms and advisors are honest, ethical and very few investors will ever experience any type of fraud in their lifetime. That having been said, however, I still urge those of you reading this book to use caution when it comes to money matters, and keep an eye on your assets, regardless of where they are invested. It just makes good sense to do so.

Preventing Fraud

These are several simple steps we can take that will protect us from financial fraud. Many of them are so simple that you may do a double take. But it will make you a better steward of your financial affairs.

Open your statements and look at them. You would be amazed at the number of people I encounter who tell me they don't like opening their account statements. This is especially true during times of market volatility when statements from brokerage houses and account custodians may contain bad news.

"I'm afraid to open them," said one woman, who said she just puts them in order of postmark with a rubber band around them and opens the one she gets at the end of the year.

How are you going to know if there has been any unwarranted activity in your accounts if you don't look at them?

Review your statements. After opening your statements, review them promptly. Look at the balance first. If it is lower, seek to understand why it is lower. If you don't understand your statement, call the bank, custodian, or brokerage firm, and ask questions until you do understand. Keep a file on each account and organize your statements by month, and then keep a separate hanging folder for each year.

Look for unexplained checks or bank transfers, unauthorized debits or credit card purchases you don't think you made. We sometimes give access to our accounts without knowing it.

If you use a computer, get online access and compare your paper statement with what you see online. It is not unheard of for those handling accounts to create fake paper statements to cover up fraud. Comparing the online statements with the paper statements is an easy way to detect this.

Call and verify. If all does not seem well with your account, call the custodian, bank, insurance company or brokerage firm from which your statements originate, and ask them to verify the balance and explain any discrepancy to your satisfaction. Even if there is no problem, it is a good idea to do this once a year. If you don't understand your investments, get a second opinion. Ask questions until you understand.

If it *sounds* too good to be true it probably is. If you are promised returns that no one else seems to be getting on their investments, that is a huge red flag. Get a second opinion from other professionals, such as CPAs, attorneys, or a knowledgeable family member or family friend as a sounding board. If you are not comfortable with the explanation you are receiving, contact a knowledgeable, trusted professional for assistance.

Never make checks payable to an individual. Unless you are paying a handyman for household repairs, or the people who mow the lawn for you, never make checks payable, or give large sums of cash to an individual. If a business transaction is legitimate, the check will always be made to a company, custodian, brokerage firm, insurance company or bank, not an advisor or an advisory firm. The exception to this is when the advice is understood to be offered in exchange for a fee and that understanding is made up front.

Credit Card Fraud is on the rise. Here are some practical DOs and DON'Ts:
Do:
- Open your bill and look at it. Report any unauthorized charges right away, both by telephone and by e-mail or letter.
- Keep copies of all correspondence regarding disputed charges until the matter is resolved.
- When you are at a cash register using your card, don't let the card out of your sight, and get it back as quickly as possible.
- Save all receipts. Compare them with what's on the monthly statement.
- Sign the back of your cards, and put your picture on them if that service is available.
- Keep a record of your account numbers, their expiration dates, and the phone number and address of each company in a secure place.
- Destroy all carbons immediately.
- Draw a line through any blank spaces above the total. Don't draw a zero, which could easily be altered.

Don't:
- Leave credit cards lying around. Either activate them, or cut them up.
- Lend your card to anyone.
- Ever sign a blank receipt. It's like signing a blank check.
- Give out your account number over the phone unless you're doing business with a company you're sure of.
- Write your account number on the outside of an envelope.

Chances are you will never experience financial fraud in your lifetime. But the key is to be vigilant and aware. I love the line from Joseph Heller in the book, *Catch 22* – "Just because you're paranoid doesn't mean they aren't after you." Or maybe my mother said it best: "It's a game. You have money in your pocket, and everyone around you is trying to get it out."

"It's a Jungle Out There..."

The name of the radio talk show that I host, "Financial Safari," was inspired by an observation a client made while he was visiting my office with a tale of woe. He told me that he had changed jobs a few years ago but had neglected to roll over his 401(k), as was his prerogative. He said he meant to do it, but it wasn't "all that much money" and after a while, he got wrapped up in work and just forgot about it.

"I just didn't pay any attention," he said. "I just assumed it was in competent hands."

At some point, while with his previous employer, he had chosen to allocate more than half of his portfolio to high-risk growth stocks. Then, long after he had left the company, a sudden market downturn caused him to lose almost half the value of his account, or around $11,000. While that figure did not represent a vast portion of his overall savings, and thus not a huge loss, it was enough to get the man's attention. He vowed from that moment on to pay more attention to the details of his personal finances. When discussing the loss with me, he said with a slow shake of his head, "It's a jungle out there, Pete."

For the rest of that day, I thought about how many bright people there are in the world that just aren't particularly savvy when it comes to handling money. There are brilliant doctors and scientists who are right now hovering over microscopes, finding ways to prevent and cure diseases, the names of which I probably couldn't pronounce. But for all their genius and talent, they know little about market trends or income planning strategies. There are educators who have stacks of diplomas and degrees, but who couldn't pass a 25-question true and false test on estate planning basics. I wondered how many engineers and architects are there, who can calculate the load-bearing capacity of a suspension bridge, but don't know the difference between a large cap and a small cap stock?

That's what made me think of a safari. In my mind, a safari is a trek through unfamiliar territory, in pursuit of a goal. If our goal is to have that ridiculously reliable retirement income plan, as the title of this book lightheartedly suggests, then we are on a safari of sorts. We have to make our way toward that goal while treading uncharted territory, where the terrain is full of pitfalls to avoid and predators to watch out for. In the old jungle movies I used to watch as a boy, there was always a guide who knew how to lead his party through the morass of vines and scary predators. These guides always wore pith helmets and khakis, a detail that still puzzles me. But it is my opinion that a competent financial advisor should be like those guides. I don't mean that they should wear khakis and a pith helmet. I mean that their job is to lead people through the confusing financial jungle, with all of its potential hazards and pitfalls, to protect them from money-handling missteps, and help them reach their goal of a worry-free retirement.

Finding a Reliable Guide

The times in which we live have been called the "information explosion" era. We have access to unlimited information about just about everything, including how to manage our money. The problem is not that we don't have enough advice floating around out there; it's that we have too much. It's like playing a sport and having 15 coaches on the sidelines, all shouting out different instructions on what to do with the ball. It's overwhelming. There is an old saying – "Opinions are like noses; everybody has one." That is certainly true when it comes to financial advice. If you want to see all those opinions in living color, just type in the words, "financial advice" into the Google search bar and, before you can blink your eyes twice, about 400,000,000 responses will pop up. You couldn't read them all in a lifetime.

The first order of business in finding the right financial advice is to narrow the search. Just deal with information that is relevant to you and your unique, individual financial goals. Secondly, carefully inspect the credibility, reliability and capability of the ones giving the advice. It is easy for an individual to set up a website these days, or obtain "certification" from a website and hang out a shingle saying he or she is an expert. That doesn't mean they are qualified to give advice to you on how to manage your money, especially if you are in or nearing retirement.

If you are considering working with a financial advisor, make sure you obtain satisfactory proof of his or her education and training. If you are retiring, ask about the financial advisor's experience in working with retirees and his philosophy about safety versus risk.

A competent financial advisor will rarely make a recommendation to you at your first meeting. He or she will spend most of the time during the first interview listening, not talking. A competent advisor will want to fully understand your unique, individual circumstances before proceeding. Just like the lesson learned from Aesop's fable of the tortoise and the hare, slow and steady wins the race when it comes to building, maintaining and preserving our wealth. If you are urged to take *immediate* action on a strategy that promises big, quick returns, run the other way.

Don't Be Crippled by Indecision

Sometimes, you can be too cautious. Sometimes, deciding not to decide is the worst decision you can make. Taking decisive action after you have done your due diligence is on the "do" list of just about every success coach out there from Stephen Covey to Tony Robbins. One of the best stories I have ever heard to illustrate the point, however, comes from Zig Ziglar in his landmark self-help book, *See You at the Top*. In his inimitable homespun style, Zig tells the story of the cook who brought out a pan of biscuits that were no bigger than a silver dollar. When Zig asked what happened to the biscuits, the cook laughed and said, "Well, those biscuits squatted to rise, but they just got cooked in the squat."

The point he was making was that unless and until you do something with what you have learned, you might as well not have learned it. Just like those biscuits, some people are always getting ready to take action. They are almost ready to make some decisions and establish a course of action. And like those biscuits, they fail to rise because they never get past their good intentions. I second that notion. I have seen individuals squander opportunities because they wanted to collect one more opinion and gather one more report or have one more analysis run of an ever changing body of data. I don't know who came up with the expression, but I like it – "paralysis by analysis." At some point, the line shifts from prudent caution to outright procrastination, which becomes the thief of our time and thereby our resources.

When it comes to putting a retirement plan into place, time has a tendency to bend. Time is literally money in this case. When we are young, planning is just as important as it is when we are in our middle years, but because time is a slow moving stream, we don't sense the current at that age. But time is flowing just the same. By the time we reach our middle years, every month that goes by without our having a plan in place costs us, not then, but down the road. That cost compounds as we near retirement age. Why? Through our inaction, we are failing to put the "time value of money" to work for us.

On Sept 11, 2001, when the hijacked jet airliner hit the North Tower of the World Trade Center in New York City, many people in the other tower knew instinctively that it was time to get out. Some began taking immediate action to leave their offices and put as much distance as they could between themselves and trouble, whatever its cause. It was not immediately clear what had happened. But they had collected enough information to know that all was not right and that it was time to move.

Others were unsure and decided to wait and see. What if it was just an accident and everything was under control. Some well-meaning souls advised people to stay put and that there was no cause for alarm. Then the South Tower was hit and many of those people lost their lives. Some of those who procrastinated until they had more information died while they were pondering what to do.

Thus, in order to preserve your financial life, it is important to collect enough information to make a sound decision, but it is important to balance that with understanding the time value of money. Otherwise, you can just become a professional information gatherer and miss the point of why you are collecting it.

Knowledge, Understanding and Wisdom

I have heard the difference between the three perceptive cousins, knowledge, understanding and wisdom, described this way:

Knowledge is a collection of facts. You know that you are standing on a train track. You know about trains, that they are made of steel and move very fast. You know that this train is approaching the spot in which you are standing and that it is moving very swiftly. Those are facts.

Understanding is the capacity to put two and two together, so to speak. You understand the relationship between one particle of knowledge and another particle of knowledge. You understand that steel is hard. You understand that tissue is soft. You understand that if hard steel, moving fast, impacts on soft tissue, you're a goner.

Wisdom is taking the appropriate action under the circumstances. Here, it would be altogether appropriate to get off the tracks.

The point is that collecting knowledge is important. Never make an uninformed decision when it comes to money. Understanding what we learn as it relates to *our* retirement and *our* income needs is crucially important too. But all the knowledge in the world won't help us, and neither will understanding that knowledge, if we don't wisely take action on what we know and understand to be accurate and true.

Consider the Source

Where you get your information from is important. It reminds me of a commercial where the doctor, who is not a doctor, performs an operation. When everyone discovers he is not a doctor, he brightens and informs them that what gave him the confidence to do things that were outside his sphere of knowledge and experience was the fact that he stayed at a particular hotel the night before.

The commercial is clever. But what is not so funny is when people who have no idea what they are talking about pass out financial advice and, in so doing, put the financial lives of others in jeopardy. Well-meaning relatives and good friends can be the worst when it comes to this. They will sometimes offer hot stock tips they heard at work, and are adamant that this or that strategy is a sure bet. They sound so confident of it that you are a fool not to follow their counsel. Why, you would think they had spent months researching it, when, if the truth were known, it is mere rumor and speculation.

When it comes to that kind of advice, allow me to suggest building an information source tree. Find out where the information came from and see if you can nail down the original source. There is a game that my six year old daughter plays known as "telephone" where people sit in a circle and whisper a phrase into the ear of the person next to them. The humor comes when the phrase is written down and read, first as it originated, and then as what it had become after having been repeated a number of times. "No, I didn't say to *short* petroleum futures. I said to purchase shares of *off-shore* petroleum for the future!"

More often than not, when you track it down to its roots, you find that there is no starting place. Like so many things, it is just going around. Some financial advice is like that. It's an impulse with no beginning, unfounded and floating in the wind. It would be funny if it weren't so harmful. I once heard it called "taking advice from a pronoun – *they*."

As in, "Where did you say you heard that?"

"Well that's what '*they*' said."

How Will I Feel About My Decision Later?

Suzy Welch, in her book, *10-10-10: A Life Transforming Idea,* suggests this test when it comes to making decisions – Ask yourself how you will feel about your decision in 10 minutes? In 10 months? In 10 years?

Of course, with some decisions, there is no way of knowing how you will feel years from now. But it does make you think. Take having children for example. Babies are so cute and cuddly. But getting up repeatedly at all hours of the night is no fun. Then comes teething, followed by the "terrible twos." Child rearing is a delight, but it is also an awesome responsibility. It is difficult for a young couple contemplating raising a family to imagine all of the difficulties that accompany the joys. But at least asking the how-will-I-feel questions forces them to think. Imagining that precious bundle of joy you bring home from the hospital as anything but a cooing little baby is a mental stretch. But if you are going to really "count the cost," you must at least try.

"I wouldn't take a million dollars for any one of my three children," said one man about his teenagers. "But I wouldn't give you a nickel for another one."

When it comes to large purchases and decisions involving money management, invoking the 10-10-10 rule may not be a bad idea. If you have reservations, by all means clear them up. Get second opinions. Consult with others until your yellow lights either turn red or green. If the lights are red, then stop. Pick a new course. If your lights are green, that's a signal to go ahead and make a decision. Inaction and indecision when something is right for you can be just as damaging to your wealth as the wrong kind of action.

CHAPTER FIFTEEN

One Size Does Not Fit All

*"If you only have a hammer, you have a tendency to see
every problem as a nail"* – Abraham Maslow

Y ou will sometimes see the tag "one size fits all" on cheap baseball caps. That's because they have that little plastic gizmo on the back that has several adjustments on it. Other than that, I can't really think of a case where one size really does fit all, or where I want it to fit anything on me. I guess I am spoiled. I like my things tailor-made…just for me.

If you are dealing with a financial advisor who sells products, you might end up with a one-size-fits-all financial plan. I recommend that you find an advisor who doesn't sell products, but one who finds solutions. Since you are unique and your goals, aspirations, dreams and your asset picture are unique, the holistic financial planner will have to "measure you" first before he can prescribe a plan. That is, he or she will have to find out what your goals are, what your current financial situation is, and then prepare a plan that will get you where you want to go and keep you there for life. It will take some individual "measuring" to prepare the tailor-made financial plan you really need. There is no "one size fits all" when it comes to financial planning.

Measuring

When I was a boy, buying a new pair of shoes was a once a year ritual, but my mother was always diligent in seeing to it that we had sturdy shoes that fit us well. Our job was to take care of them and make sure that we did not grow more than one shoe size per year - a biological feat that I was somehow able to pull off.

The first thing we did when we visited the shoe store was sit in a special chair for trying on shoes. Then the shoe salesman would come over with a large metal device for measuring feet. I would place my right foot into the metal tray, and the salesman would have me stand, establishing the length of my foot. Then he would slide a metal caliper up to the ball of my foot and take a measurement giving him my foot's width. He would then disappear into a room and come back with several boxes containing pairs of shoes that matched my shoe size. It was unthinkable for the process to end with merely selecting a style and color, however. The shoes had to be tried on. Just going on the basis of size could fool you. All shoes were made just a little differently, and two shoes the same size could fit differently. Since the shoes had to last a year, my mother instructed us to allow for a little room for growth in our assessment of the fit, which I did. The point is, the shoes fit, and we knew that by the way they felt on our feet.

Sometimes you can just sense when financial advice is right for you. Trust that instinct. There is a reason why you feel that way. If you are seeking guarantees, and yet nowhere in your proposal do you hear or see the word "guarantee," then trust that instinct. Ask questions. Get another opinion before committing to a plan of action that doesn't fit.

Conflicting Opinions

It is just as possible to receive conflicting financial advice as it is to receive conflicting medical advice. That doesn't necessarily mean that the recommendations of one doctor are evil and ill-intentioned and that the other doctor is all-seeing, all-knowing and all-wise. It probably means that one doctor was educated in one approach to the treatment of ailments, and the other doctor was educated in another. While the opinions may conflict, they may both have validity.

I have a friend who visited a doctor who told him that he had developed high blood pressure and was to begin taking two medications right away. My friend is one who eschews any kind of pill as a toxic substance. He rarely has a headache, but when he does, he says he prefers to "just wait it out" and refuses any offer of aspirin. So you can imagine the push back the doctor got from him when he heard the proposed remedy.

My friend booked an appointment with another doctor for a second opinion. Doctor #2 told him that it would be a mistake to start taking medicine without trying a more natural approach. Doctor #2 put my friend on a program of diet and exercise and, after losing 25 pounds in the next three months, his blood pressure returned to normal.

Which doctor was right? They both were. They just approached the same problem from two different points of view. But which doctor's advice fit the patient the best? The advice of doctor #2.

It's the same way with financial advice. One professional may be trained in building wealth, but not in preserving it and distributing it during retirement. Naturally, that advisor's recommendations will lean heavily in the direction of solutions that carry more risk, such as stocks, bonds and mutual funds. After all, that is his or her area of expertise and training. Recommendations from that advisor can only reflect what is found in his or her area of scope and focus.

On the other hand, advisors who specialize in retirement income planning are more likely to reflect the spirit of caution and risk aversion displayed by most seniors. When they are making their recommendations, they will generally lean toward financial products and strategies where risk is kept to a minimum and more guarantees can be found.

Is it possible for greed to motivate those in the financial profession? Sure it is. Greed was behind scandals involving Bernie Madoff and Ivan Boesky. If the greed virus infects a financial advisor, causing him or her to make recommendations strictly because of fees, commissions, or other forms of remuneration, then shame on them. That would be like a doctor prescribing medicine for a kickback from the pharmaceutical company that made the pills. Such things are rare, that's why they make headlines.

As it is in the medical community, polarized opinions among financial professionals are more the result of education and training, not greed. This explains why you may get different solutions to the same problem. Like divergent pathways that ultimately lead to the same destination, it is not uncommon to encounter two opposing schools of thought, each with its own validity. The main thing to make sure of is that the recommendation you choose is a *good fit for you.*

If the Shoe Fits...

We know when we have the wrong size shoe on. And we don't need a measuring device. Our feet will scream it to us. If someone tells us that a size 8 would look good on us and we happen to wear a size 10, we wouldn't heed that advice, for obvious reasons. In the financial world, we need to explore ideas until we have a plan that fits us well. To do otherwise may be harmful to our wealth.

Finding the Right Size for You

One way to tell if you are dealing with an advisor who is limited in his or her scope of training and experience is by looking at your statement. If you have several mutual funds and they are all from the same mutual fund family, you are likely dealing with an agent of a firm, not an unbiased fiduciary. If an advisor specializes in one product and one product only, then we can expect that any recommendation we receive will be based around that one product family. Frankly, that makes about as much sense as going to a shoe store that features only one size and style of shoe. I love the maxim of Psychology Professor Abraham Maslow, "When the only tool you have is a hammer, every problem begins to resemble a nail."

The meaning is clear. If your knowledge or training is limited to one type of solution, then you will choose that solution for every problem you encounter, even if another approach may be more effective.

Another way to tell if we are being advised by someone limited in their scope and focus is to observe the interview process they conduct. Do they begin the relationship by asking many introspective questions – the kind that elicits from us the nature of our dreams and the details of our goals and the exact measure of our capacity to accomplish them? Or do they spend most of their time convincing us that one particular company or product is the answer. Just as with the shoes, the time spent measuring is important. It is essential to the decision-making process. We must know clearly how the plan will:

- Provide for our future income needs
- Provide for our heirs after we are gone
- Compensate for inflation

If we ask those questions and fail to receive an answer that seems right to us, then we may wish to seek another opinion.

Fit is Important

An Armani suit that doesn't fit you well is just cloth. A financial plan that doesn't fit you well is just paper, words and figures, even if it is accompanied by charts and graphs. If it doesn't fit you, it could be like the football helmets that were issued to me in the fifth grade. They were ill-fitting and offered little protection.

My head had something to do with it, of course. The coach said it was "too small." Luckily, I never took a good hit. In those days, helmets were "one size fits all" with a few adjustments possible with the straps, if you could figure them out. Today's helmets have inflatable padding so that the helmets fit the exact configuration of the player's head. The snug fit is designed to keep injuries to a minimum.

When it comes to accepting and following a financial plan, you should expect a good fit, especially if you are approaching retirement. You need one that gives you the peace of mind that you deserve – one that allows for growth and preserves your wealth so that you do not run out of money as you live through your retirement.

Why Not Get It In Writing?

Here's an idea. If you are presented a plan for retirement that you wish to be constructed in such a way that it will preserve your wealth and guarantee that you will not run out of money, regardless of how long you live, why not have it in writing and signed by your financial planner. Wouldn't that be a true litmus test as to the plan's validity?

"Dear Mr. and Mrs. Client. I do so solemnly swear that the plan I have presented to you on this date shall preserve the funds you have accumulated thus far and provide you with an income as specified herein that you cannot outlive."

Why not? If your planner refuses to sign a simple statement, it could be that they do not know that strategies exist that would support such a promise. In that case, you should seek help from another planner.

CHAPTER SIXTEEN

Lifetime Income Is Possible and Necessary

"When I was young, I thought that money
was the most important thing in life;
now that I am old, I know that it is." – Oscar Wilde

W hen 401(k) programs began replacing traditional pension plans in the early 1990s, the masses thought it was a great idea. After all, employees got to manage their own money. The 1990s rocked when it came to returns. Workers thought that 10% annual returns would continue for life. This sure beat the pants off the old pension plans, which locked them into a fixed income for life. Employers were happy too. They found pension plans costly. This was their ticket out. They were all too happy to provide matching funds. After all, it was a corporate tax write off and, with plan statements showing increasing balances during the 1990s, companies were engendering positive employee relations. Those in the legislature who created the groundwork for defined contribution retirement plans, thought they had come up with an answer to happy retirement.

Today, there is no such euphoria over 401(k)s as the pathway to a secure retirement among employees, and some experts are beginning to feel that the experiment was all a big mistake.

What's the problem? There are several.
- Many employees don't contribute enough to their plan.
- Employees experience a financial emergency, borrow from their plans and don't repay the loans.

- Too many people take early distributions and get hit with penalties and taxes.
- With employees able to make their own investment choices, many try unsuccessfully to time the market.
- When companies hit hard times, some eliminate their matching programs.
- 401(k) plans don't provide guaranteed incomes. When your money runs out, it's gone.

Of course, none of this would be an issue had the stock market not gone into a coma during the decade of the 2000s. All of this, right when the baby boomers were getting ready to retire, too. All that did was cause new levels of concern. According to the Employee Benefits Research Institute, more than 50% of Americans have less than $25,000 saved for retirement.

What a Retirement Plan Should Do

For a retirement income plan to be worth its salt, it should provide (a) income you can't outlive, and (b) cover expenses you can't live without, like healthcare and housing. This is one of the reasons why many retirees are turning portions of their underperforming 401(k) retirement accounts into income annuities, which allows for a portion of your retirement savings to become a stream of income, guaranteed for as long as you (and in some cases your spouse) live.

Even with a conservative withdrawal strategy from an equities based retirement fund, you may run out of money in your lifetime, because there are no guarantees.

Why the 4% Rule No Longer Works

For decades, the conventional wisdom on Wall Street has been to follow the 4% rule when it comes to income during retirement. This strategy typically suggests that you park your savings in an equities based account and withdraw 4% per year and then rebalance the account each year, using a 60%-40% mixture of stocks and bonds throughout a 30-year period.

When you do the math, in order to have a $40,000 per year income, you would have to start with $1 million. That's a problem. Most people don't have a million-dollar nest egg. I understand the idea behind the theory, but it only works when the market behaves well. Lately, that has not been the case. Also, with life expectancy on the rise, who's to say that 30 years is enough? One more thing, nothing is guaranteed. I think this is one reason why seniors are seeking out the income annuities. The dollar amounts are guaranteed.

The truth is, the economic landscape is constantly changing. What worked 20 years ago just doesn't work today. What worked two years ago, might not work today. If an income that you cannot outlive is not built into a retirement plan, then it is not a retirement plan. It should have a financial cruise control feature, or it's not a retirement plan. It's a wish. It's a hope. It's what might happen instead of what will happen.

Summary
Baby Step Six: Getting The Right Kind of Help

Be Careful with your money; you may need it someday! People who believe in honesty and fair dealing, vastly outnumber those who are motivated by greed and selfishness. But since the latter are still in the world, keep an eye out for the shysters and the charlatans. Ever since money was invented, there have been those whose specialty it is to remove it from your possession. It could even be a company draining your account with too many fees or fees that are too high. Pay attention to your accounts. Open your statements. Understand them or ask questions until you do. Hidden charges are just that – charges that you didn't knowingly agree to that are poorly displayed in your statements on purpose, in the hopes that you won't see them.

When it comes to financial planning, there is a Tsunami of information flooding the airwaves and the print media. Well-meaning friends and relatives want to give you advice. All of this can be confusing. Some throw their hands up, wondering which course to take. Sadly, every profession has its share of those without the knowledge or expertise to practice in that area, and the financial profession is no exception. A competent financial advisor will have the proper credentials, just like any true professional. But what is even more important is experience and capability to specialize in solving problems unique to you. Don't allow the abundance of information, some of which seems contradictory, to make you a victim of indecision. Deciding not to decide can be harmful to your wealth. Trust yourself. You know when answers fit and when they don't.

If you are retiring, you need a financial plan that has a guaranteed lifetime income. Don't settle for projections and maybes. If you don't hear and read the word "guarantee" in the plan, get a second opinion.

Step Seven

Teaching the Next Generation

CHAPTER SEVENTEEN

Leaving the Right Kind of Legacy

"We don't inherit the earth from our ancestors;
we borrow it from our children."
David Brower

Ray Bradbury, world famous science fiction writer who died June 5, 2012, was well known for inserting bits of his personal philosophy into the dialogue of his novels. In *Fahrenheit 451,* published in 1953, he has one of the characters imparting this bit of wisdom about leaving a legacy:

"Everyone must leave something behind when he dies . . . Something your hand touched some way so your soul has somewhere to go when you die . . . It doesn't matter what you do, so long as you change something from the way it was before you touched it into something that's like you after you take your hands away."

What a beautiful sentiment! It is only natural for us to wish to leave behind something of value for those we love, even if it is no more than something for which they will remember us. But, if we have the means, how much better it would be to put in place a provision that would enhance their lives. We want to make sure that our grandchildren have a college education. As they grow older, we want them to be in a position to own their own home and be able to pay for it.

When it comes to setting up a legacy for young people, doing it such a way that they can't blow the money out of youthful exuberance is important. The touchy subject of irresponsible children often comes up when I meet with clients wishing to provide a legacy for their children and grandchildren.

"We have four children," began one couple. "Three are responsible adults, and the fourth, the youngest, can't keep a quarter in his pocket."

They told me that they only wanted what was best for their children, and they were worried that the youngest son would squander it as soon as he received it.

"Are we wrong to think that way," asked the wife?

It was a legitimate question. They said they wished they could treat all of their children alike and that they didn't want to hurt their son's feelings.

A major portion of their legacy assets was contained in an IRA that the couple had spent most of their lives building. I told them that they were probably doing their son a big favor by doing some extra planning to protect their spendthrift son from his own inclinations. I assured them that they could set up their estate in such a way that all would be well served. I showed them how they could set up a spendthrift trust with the one son in mind and "stretch" the IRA so that (a) the value could transfer to the children and then the grandchildren and beyond, (b) quadruple in value over time and (c) avoid excessive taxation. They were surprised to learn how much could be accomplished for the long term good of their loved ones, with just a little planning.

Stretch IRAs

Stretch IRAs are no secret, and they are not a new type of IRA. It is simply a method of transferring wealth that allows you to "stretch" the proceeds from the account over several future generations. Most IRA owners know that tax law requires that individual retirement account holders begin taking out at least minimum amounts, known as required minimum distributions, or RMDs, from their accounts once they reach age 70 ½. The amounts are based on the IRS life expectancy table. It's pretty obvious why the IRS wants you to start drawing down these accounts when you get older. After all, your money sat in those accounts, tantalizingly out of their reach while it accrued tax-deferred earnings. If you are fortunate enough to inherit someone else's IRA, you will be required to take minimum distributions each year from the IRA account based on your life expectancy figure - regardless of your age.

Here's where the "stretch" comes in. At the death of the owner, IRA accounts are passed on to the designated beneficiary. Most IRA owners name their spouse as their beneficiary and their children as contingent beneficiaries. There's nothing wrong with that. But it might require the surviving spouse to take more taxable income from the IRA than he or she really needs. If income needs are not an issue, then naming younger beneficiaries, such as grandchildren and great grandchildren, allows you to stretch the value of the IRA out over generations. Why? Because the RMD for a youngster will be a fraction of what it would be for an older person. The proceeds are doled out in smaller amounts for a longer period of time. This allows the money to continue to grow, tax deferred. The effects of compound, tax-free growth are startling when you plug them into a calculator.

It confounds me why more financial planners aren't aware of how to stretch an IRA. All that is required is a little paperwork. And yet, a blank look comes over the faces of many a financial professional when you ask them about it. Ed Slott, one of the nation's premier experts in the field of stretch IRAs, makes the point that if we don't make an effort to take care of our families in such a way, we will end up leaving the majority of our inheritance to Uncle Sam. There are many ways to avoid paying more than your fair share of taxes that are perfectly legal. In many cases, the details of how to go about implementing these strategies are contained in the IRS code manuals.

Many love the concept of stretching their IRAs strictly from a sentimental point of view.

"I get a little choked up thinking about my great-granddaughter receiving a check each year on her birthday when I'm long gone," said one client. The check would, of course, be the RMD paid out of an IRA that the man had started funding decades earlier.

Can you pass on the proceeds of your IRA to your loved ones in the form of a lump sum? Sure you can. But the beneficiary of a lump sum will have a whopper of a tax bill and, depending on his or her sense of thrift, may have a challenge not to spend the money irresponsibly. Setting up an income legacy to heirs is growing in popularity for obvious reasons.

Buying Life Insurance with the RMDs?

On one particular radio show, I asked the caller to give the producer his number. I wanted to call him back and calm him down off the air. He had just turned 70 ½ and discovered that he had no choice in the matter of taking his RMDs. To his way of thinking, the government was forcing him to take money out of an account that he had set aside for his son. He was not super wealthy, but he had plenty of income and did not need the money from the RMDs.

"Are you healthy?" I asked him.

"As a horse," he said.

"What if you took the RMD, which you don't need anyway, and used it to pay the premiums on a life insurance policy on you, with your son as beneficiary."

The silence that ensued told me that the gears in his mind were turning.

"Can I do that?" he said.

"All day long," I replied.

The amount of life insurance he purchased using that simple concept was $250,000. The policy he purchased came with a long-term care attachment. He was happy as a clam.

Life insurance is viewed by some as merely income replacement for a working family member who dies prematurely. Perhaps that's all it was at one time, but in this modern financial world, life insurance has become an important cog in the works of leaving a legacy. You can leave a tax-free death benefit and set it up in a way that will provide a yearly payment while the balance continues to grow. Each time they get that check, they will think of you. That's leaving a legacy. It's all in the way you structure your financial affairs.

It's only natural that we want our children and grandchildren to have a better life than we did. I have talked to a lot of parents who have seen their children through college and watched them grow into adults with successful financial lives. You can tell by talking to them that their passion is not so much to fatten the bank accounts of their immediate children so much as it is to see that their grandchildren are well cared for.

I want them to remember who grandma and grandpa are," one woman said.

When our grandchildren get older and develop a greater capacity for understanding just what kind of character their grandparents and great-grandparents possessed, then they too will have a sense of legacy, and we will have contributed to it more than we can know. They may need our help in the world they inherit. It may be that their hurdles will be a bit higher than ours, and their dreams not as achievable without our help.

Dividend Reinvestment Programs

Here's an idea: Pre-fund a pension for your grandchildren. Right now, you can start putting money away that will give them a lifetime income when they retire. You can start a "drip plan" today and wait for some milestone in their life to present it as a gift for them. Dividend Reinvestment Programs are an excellent way of doing this. Each month, deduct $100 or $200 – some predetermined amount – from your checking account, and use it to buy shares of stock in a company that produces dividends. Each and every month, on the same day of the month, the money coming out of that account will buy whatever number of shares that amount can buy that day. If the stock price is down, it will buy more shares. If the stock price is up, the money will buy fewer shares. But dollar cost averaging will see you through. You are averaging your cost over the lifetime of the program and plowing the gains back into it. When the company issues dividends, you buy more shares of the stock. It is an excellent way to leave a legacy and teach your children and grandchildren the value of money and the principles of investing.

When I was in high school, I started one of these programs using McDonalds and Exxon. The little secret here is, you don't want the stock to do too well at first. You want it to stay in business obviously, but you want it to stay relatively low when you are buying it. That way you can own more shares. When you select a company that you know will be around for a long time, you will see the value of the company increase as the years go by. Whether you give the program as a legacy, or you use it for your own retirement, you will eventually have something that will fund the period known as "reverse dollar cost averaging." That's when you are selling shares of stock as you withdraw cash from the account on an incremental basis.

No Excuses

I once attended a seminar where the motivational speaker issued this indictment to the audience: "We are great inventors of excuses. We are turning into a generation of blamers and excuse makers. If we could spend half the time actually doing the things we are thinking up excuses for not doing, it would be amazing how much we could accomplish." That put me to thinking. I ran down the mental checklist of my own procrastinations, and I had to admit that the speaker was right. We do have a tendency to put things off. It's only human nature. See, I just did it again!

"Roll up your sleeves and put your shoulder to the wheel and your nose to the grindstone," he continued. "Make a plan and stick to it. The only one you really have to blame is the one whose thumbs are pointing back at you when you put your elbows up at 90 degree angles like this."

He placed his arms in a position where his thumbs were pointing back at himself. Then he pointed his finger at the audience.

"Remember, when you point the finger at someone else, there are three others pointing back at you."

"Make a plan and stick to it," he had said. Naturally, I thought of a financial plan, although I don't think that was necessarily what he had in mind. I wondered how many people were putting off getting on track with a workable financial plan and what excuses they might come up with for their procrastination. According to the speaker, most people will spend more time planning their next vacation than they will planning how they'll spend the rest of their lives. I think he's right. It seems to be that acting in our own behalf is sometimes the most difficult act to perform.

REFERENCES USED IN THE BOOK

Book References:
- David Schwartz's book, *How much is a Million*, was written in Published October 22nd 1993 by HarperCollins
- *The Little Engine that Could* was written by Arnold Monk in 1930.
- Virginia Morrison *How to Care for Aging Parents: A Complete Guide* 1996
- Zig Ziglar *See you at the Top* - published in 1975 by the Pelican Publishing Company
- Suzy Welsh *10- 10- 10: A Life Transforming Idea* was published April 14, 2009.

Movie References:
- *Apollo 13* - Written by Jim Lovell and Jeffrey Kluger; Published in 1994

ABOUT THE AUTHOR

Pete D'Arruda:
The Right Coach For The Retirement Game

While most students in college are content to let scholarships, grants, or even parents pay tuition, Pete D'Arruda was not interested in taking any hand-outs.

After his first semester, Pete decided it was best to pay his own way rather than depending on anyone else.

"It was a lot harder, but I learned the power of money," he says about the multiple jobs taken on to fund his higher education. "I did everything from delivering pizza to writing parking tickets."

Where does this valuable sense of independence come from? Well, the man who his current clients know fondly as Coach Pete, was managing paper routes at the tender age of 7. Even then, he learned the downside of the business trade.

"I had to pay the newspaper for the papers, and then collect from people," he jokes. "Sometimes, my clients thought they were stiffing the paper, but they were stiffing me!"

Always quick with a joke but quicker with an unrelenting dedication to his clients, D'Arruda continued to forge his own path in college where he decided to become a financial adviser, surprisingly against his father's wishes.

See, his father received his Ph.D. in Physics and wanted Pete to follow in his footsteps. Even though financial advising is hardly a flippant profession, D'Arruda had some major shoes to fill, with his father excelling as a top professor in North Carolina. Pete's clients will tell you, he filled those shoes pretty darn well!

"While my father was studying triangles and equations, my equation was

'How can we build as much money for folks as possible, and do it safely?'" he says.

His solution to this equation – <u>Capital Financial Advisory Group</u>, which he founded in Cary, NC.

The firm specializes in pre-retirees and retirees, a demographic that includes people in their late 50s, 60s, 70s, and even early 80s. The first thing D'Arruda does when meeting with a client is to dig deep and find out where they are financially.

"Most people don't know where they stand now. They spread out all of these statements they've collected over the years, and ask, 'What should I be doing?'" "We have to figure out exactly what they have and decide whether or not to continue on the same path or change directions."

For Pete, managing money is like sitting in the upper deck of a hockey game. It's only from that viewpoint where one can really see the big picture.

"We take a financial satellite view of what they can't see on the ground. People brag about being right down on the field, but you can't really see anything from there," he jokes. "The only good thing at that level is that you can smell the players."

For D'Arruda and Capital Financial, a successful retirement is all about customization. Each individual is different and has a unique set of needs, goals, and priorities. Pete doesn't believe in the one-size-fits-all equation.

"A lot of these companies you see on TV want to give you a cookie cutter portfolio. They pull a portfolio off the shelf and say, 'You're 55, here you go,'" he says. "That's just not planning! Whose retirement are they planning, yours or theirs?"

D'Arruda offers customized plans and believes in holding *at least* quarterly meetings with his clients in order to update the plan as necessary. His foremost goal is always to take the worry out of retirement so his clients can sleep well at night.

"There's going to come a time that you have 30 to 40 years of unemployment, known as retirement," he says. "Social Security is a nice little check that hopefully will come, but it's important to have supplemental plans. If you built the plans correctly, you should have increasing income."

So, where does this no-nonsense approach come from? More importantly, where does the nickname Coach Pete come from?

Pete has been in the financial services industry for more than 20 years, and he has stayed true to his beliefs from day one. He began his career as a mortgage broker in 1988. He called it a dirty business, and it was difficult, even painful, for him to watch other brokers taking advantage of clients.

Because of this, he stayed in that industry only a few years before moving to the financial assistance world in 1991. His impact was felt immediately.

With a heart bent on helping the community, Pete began his new direction, which focused on helping teachers. During that time, he also earned the title, Coach Pete. Most teachers didn't realize they were entitled to a special tax deduction, which was a part of a federal tax shelter created to help educators. For his efforts, some of those he helped went on to retire a whole year early!

"My last name was hard to pronounce so they asked if they could call me Coach Pete," he says. "I'd always visit the school, and the principal would announce that Coach Pete was coming."

The moniker stuck with him and now Pete sees himself as a financial coach, guiding a different demographic toward fiscal success.

"A team would just be a collection of players without a coach to get them organized," he explains. "That's what I do in the financial world, get clients organized. We organize and conquer the retirement equation."

Still bucking the trend, Pete focuses only on his clients' best interests. Even when most advisors might not be doing right by their clients, Pete considers his clients' wellbeing to be his responsibility.

"I have a fiduciary responsibility, which most financial professionals don't have," he says. "That means I have to put the client's needs ahead of my needs. I have to disclose anything I make. Isn't that a novel concept?"

An honest man through and through, he is shocked other advisors aren't more up front with clients. He even sees other people in the industry finding ways to get paid twice for one service. Often, the financial institution is compensating Pete, so what happens in this case? He doesn't charge the client!

It's just not about the money with Pete but about coaching his retirees to a happy and healthy future.

"I've never had a complaint in 20 years," he proudly boasts. "I have an A-plus rating with the Better Business Bureau and the National Ethics Association."

With an intense drive to place himself in his clients' shoes, D'Arruda, unlike most financial consultants, puts his money where his mouth is.

"I practice what I preach. I see people all of the time recommending crap they'd never put their own money in. Everything I recommend, I already have," he emphasizes.

In the country's current economic situation, Pete understands why it may be difficult to trust anyone in the financial industry.

"You have to look at person's track record and trust your instinct," he says. "But not making a decision is just as bad, or worse, than making a bad decision sometimes."

In fact, D'Arruda admits he's made mistakes in the past, but has learned greatly from them. This is wisdom he wants to pass on to others. His biggest lesson stems from the dot-com bubble that happened at the turn of the century.

"I made a whole lot of money day trading stocks," he adds. "It took me a couple of years to make it, and about two weeks to lose it. In the year 2000, the market didn't spring back up. That's why I'm here—to make sure your portfolio can withstand those ups and downs."

Pete can't imagine the emotional rollercoaster a senior would go through during retirement if the market were fluctuating. That's exactly why his clients love his safety-first approach to investing. If someone is heading into retirement and wants a rock-solid plan built off experience, Pete is the coach to make this happen.

Naturally, this honest and knowledgeable advisor was drawn to radio. After talking with Coach Pete for more than a minute, it becomes clear that this man is a natural communicator.

What can listeners expect from this hit broadcast? He's currently the host of "Coach Pete's Financial Safari," a weekly radio show played on stations throughout North Carolina, and the rest of the country including: Miami, Chicago, San Francisco, Boston, Richmond, Atlanta, Las Vegas and Dallas. He's on over 100 radio stations.

Pete delves into common sense financial techniques. The show's easy to understand message has become so popular that the show is expanding faster than he can update his website.

Coach Pete is also the author of three books, including "Fine Print Fiasco," "Financial Safari," and "Have you been talking to Financial Aliens?" Themes of these easy readers include helping others avoid being taken advantage of and translating financial jargon for any layman.

Seems like Coach Pete actually wants to educate and help the retiring demographic, doesn't it? In a financial world full of professionals who try to circumnavigate or mislead, everyday people can rest assured that kind, honest, and educated advisors like Pete, are still around to help.

To learn more about Capital Financial Advisory Group, visit www.SayNO-toRisk.com, or call 866-882-9785.